Y0-CPW-168

RECEPTIONS OF WAR

OKLAHOMA PROJECT FOR DISCOURSE AND THEORY

OKLAHOMA PROJECT FOR DISCOURSE
AND THEORY

SERIES EDITORS
Robert Con Davis, University of Oklahoma
Ronald Schleifer, University of Oklahoma

ADVISORY BOARD

RECEPTIONS OF WAR
VIETNAM IN AMERICAN CULTURE

BY ANDREW MARTIN

UNIVERSITY OF OKLAHOMA PRESS : NORMAN AND LONDON

Library of Congress Cataloging-in-Publication Data

Martin, Andrew, 1946–
    Receptions of war : Vietnam in American culture / by Andrew
Martin. – 1st ed.
        p.   cm. – (Oklahoma project for discourse and theory ; v. 10)
    Includes bibliographical references (p.   ) and index.
    ISBN 0-8061-2491-1 (alk. paper)
        1. Vietnamese Conflict, 1961–1975–United States. 2. Vietnam-
ese Conflict, 1961–1975–Influence. 3. Vietnamese Conflict, 1961–
1975–Motion pictures and the conflict. 4. Vietnamese Conflict,
1961–1975–Literature and the conflict. 5. United States–Civilization–1945–   I. Title. II. Series.
DS558.M4   1993
959.704'3373–dc20   92-33825
                                                              CIP

Receptions of War: Vietnam in American Culture is Volume 10 of
the Oklahoma Project for Discourse and Theory.

The paper in this book meets the guidelines for permanence and
durability of the Committee on Production Guidelines for Book
Longevity of the Council on Library Resources, Inc.

1   2   3   4   5   6   7   8   9   10

This book is dedicated to my parents,
Beryl and Walter Martin.

CONTENTS

SERIES EDITORS' FOREWORD

THE Oklahoma Project for Discourse & Theory is a series of interdisciplinary texts whose purpose is to explore the cultural institutions that constitute the human sciences, to see them in relation to one another, and, perhaps above all, to see them as products of particular discursive practices. To this end, we hope that the Oklahoma Project will promote dialogue within and across traditional disciplines—psychology, philology, linguistics, history, art history, aesthetics, logic, political economy, religion, philosophy, anthropology, communications, and the like—in texts that theoretically are located across disciplines. In recent years, in a host of new and traditional areas, there has been great interest in such discursive and theoretical frameworks. Yet we conceive of the Oklahoma Project as going beyond local inquiries, providing a larger forum for interdiscursive theoretical discussions and dialogue.

Our agenda in previous books and certainly in this one has been to present through the University of Oklahoma Press a series of critical volumes that set up a theoretical encounter among disciplines, an interchange not limited to literature but covering virtually the whole range of the human sciences. It is a critical series with an important reference in literary studies—thus mirroring the modern development of discourse theory—but including all approaches, other than quantitative studies, open to semiotic and post-semiotic analysis and to the wider concerns of cultural studies. Regardless of its particular domain, each book in the series will investigate characteristically post-Freudian, post-Saussurean, and post-Marxist questions about culture and discourses that constitute different cultural phenomena. The Oklahoma Project is a sustained dialogue intended to make a significant contribution to the contemporary understanding of the human sciences in the contexts of cultural theory and cultural studies.

The title of the series reflects, of course, its home base, the University of Oklahoma. But it also signals in a significant way the particularity of the *local* functions within historical and conceptual frameworks for understanding culture. *Oklahoma* is a haunting place-name in American culture. A Choctaw phrase meaning "red people," it goes back to the Treaty of Dancing Rabbit Creek in Mississippi in 1830. For Franz Kafka, it conjured up the idea of America itself, both the indigenous Indian peoples of North America and the vertiginous space of the vast plains. It is also the place-name, the "American" starting point, with which Wallace Stevens begins his *Collected Poems.* Historically, too, it is a place in which American territorial and political expansion was reenacted in a single day in a retracing called the Oklahoma land run. Geographically, it is the heartland of the continent.

As such—in the interdisciplinary Oklahoma Project for Discourse & Theory—we are hoping to describe, above all, multifaceted *interests* within and across various studies of discourse and culture. Such interests are akin to what Kierkegaard calls the "in-between" aspect of experience, the "inter esse," and, perhaps more pertinently, what Nietzsche describes as the always *political* functioning of concepts, art works, and language—the functioning of power as well as knowledge in discourse and theory. Such politics, occasioning dialogue and bringing together powerfully struggling and often unarticulated positions, disciplines, and assumptions, is always local, always particular. In some ways, such interests function in broad feminist critiques of language, theory, and culture as well as microphilosophical and microhistorical critiques of the definitions of truth and art existing within ideologies of "disinterested" meaning. They function in the interested examination of particular disciplines and general disciplinary histories. They function (to allude to two of our early titles) in the very interests of theory and the particularity of the postmodern age in which many of us find ourselves. In such interested particulars, we believe, the human sciences are articulated. We hope that the books of the Oklahoma Project will provide sites of such interest and that in them, individually and collectively, the monologues of traditional scholarly discourse will become heteroglosses, just as such place-names as *Oklahoma* and such commonplace words and concepts as *discourse* and *theory* can become sites for the dialogue and play of culture.

ROBERT CON DAVIS
RONALD SCHLEIFER

Norman, Oklahoma

ACKNOWLEDGMENTS

ALTHOUGH writing a book can be a lonely, even alienating experience, in the end it must be admitted that books, especially one's first book, eventually emerge from a complex of personal experiences, contemporary influences, and historical sources. *Receptions of War* is no exception, being the result of a personal and intellectual history that has evolved in and across a number of cultural and educational environments: the University of Sussex, the University of California at Santa Barbara, the University of Iowa, and now, the University of Wisconsin at Milwaukee.

Given the narrow horizon of opportunity for working-class kids in Britain in the late 1950s and early 1960s, one might say that I have been lucky. On the other hand, I never lacked for support from my family, friends, and workmates, even when they quite rightly worried about some of the strange turns my life seemed to take. One of those turns, one of the better ones, came about though a student grant from the Greater London Council—an institution that once promised to be truly of the people, but that has since been dismantled mainly because it resisted all too successfully (at least for a while) the conservative hegemony of Thatcherism. Thanks to the GLC and its progressive cultural and educational policies, I was able to attend the University of Sussex in the mid-1970s. And it was during my studies at Sussex with the late Marcus Cunliffe and others, and through friendship with Cora Kaplan and fellow students, that I found a place for myself in what had previously been an unimagined world.

In the late 1970s I undertook what was supposed to be a year of study in the United States, at the University of California at Santa Barbara. But in California I discovered another social and intellectual home that would alter not only my own vaguely assumed career objectives but also my country of residence. And although I didn't realize it at the time, the process that would result in the writing of *Receptions of War* was already set in motion as I began to experience and absorb the continuing effects of the cultural crisis brought on by the Vietnam War. Even then the war and the sixties continued to influence profoundly many aspects of daily life and campus activity in California—and the spate of films that appeared then (*Coming Home, The Deer Hunter, Apocalypse Now*) served to intensify what was already an intensely engaged debate. At the same time, my initial field of study, American literature and history, was undergoing profound changes as well, moving in directions that I hadn't anticipated as I began to meet and work with scholars from other fields. At UCSB I was introduced to the serious study of film by Professor Charles Wolfe, whose dedication to teaching and research was an inspiration that remains with me to this day. Thanks to him I became a teaching assistant in the film program, learning from and working with Janet Bergstrom, Natasa Durovicova, Thomas Elsaesser, Al LaValley, Peter Lehman, Michael Renov, and Garrett Stewart.

At the University of Iowa I discovered what to my mind was an ideal intellectual community of teachers and graduate students. In particular I owe thanks to Professors Dudley Andrew, Melba Boyd, Dennis Corrigan, Wayne Franklin, Hanno Hardt, Ellis Hawley, Rich Horwitz, Tom Lewis, Eileen Meehan (now at the University of Arizona), Sherman Paul, Shelton Stromquist, and Steve Valasky. Finally, I owe a debt of gratitude to Professor Albert Stone, who not only served as my academic advisor and dissertation chair but also encouraged and made space for my developing critical approach to American studies.

Receptions of War was refined, and in many ways rethought, at the University of Wisconsin at Milwaukee, where I now teach. I owe a special debt of gratitude to Professor

James Sappenfield, Chair of the Department of English and Comparative Literature (1985–90), and to Professor William Halloran, Dean of the College of Letters and Science, both of whom were responsible for hiring me in the first place and who have continued to encourage and support my work over the years. I am also indebted to Professor Kathleen Woodward, Director of the Center for Twentieth Century Studies, since she has not only read and commented on sections of the present study but also included me in many of the Center's activities and events, which in turn have also had a great effect on the writing of this book. As a Center Fellow in 1989–90, it was my pleasure to work closely with my colleague Professor Gregory Jay on the Center's conference of that year, "Reconstructing Cultural Criticism in America." Greg, too, has offered careful and thoughtful readings of several sections of *Receptions of War.*

My deepest and most profound thanks go to Patrice Petro, my wife, my friend, and my constant collaborator, whose unwavering support and specific contributions to my work over the past decade and more have meant more than I can possibly say here. Throughout everything and at all times Patrice has been there for me. Without her, *Receptions of War* could not have been written.

ANDREW MARTIN

Milwaukee, Wisconsin

INTRODUCTION

> It's something like fighting with someone in your
> house, with all the precious furniture around you.
> And after that stranger got out of your house, you
> looked around at the different things in your
> house—they were all broken. The war actually took
> place in our house . . . it was really a sad thing.
>
> NGUYEN NGOC HUNG, A NORTH VIETNAMESE ARMY VETERAN

THE above epigraph, with its by-now-familiar
message of pain, loss, and regret, initially entered American
culture by means of television. It now lingers on in my life in
two modes of representation: text and video. The text, which
sits on my desk as I type these words, is a transcript from the
CBS television news program *60 Minutes;* the segment from
which the quotation comes is called "The Enemy." The video
cassette is at home somewhere among the piles of video cas-
settes that have tended to grow in proportion to the length of
time it has taken me to write this book. There are other piles,
too: popular magazines, academic journals, novels, memoirs,
histories, collections of photojournalism, comics, as well as
files full of clippings and notes. All of this represents but a
fraction of what American culture is doing with and to a war
it would rather forget or remember differently, if only it could.

Thus a veteran of the Vietnam War ("one of theirs") grieves
over the waste and destruction that American foreign policy
and firepower visited upon his country. His words emerge
from the lived experience and material actualities of a historical event, although they represent merely a fragment of that

history, which now circulates amid the flurry of Vietnam War representations and texts. His words are signs of a catastrophe that continue to affect us years after the event itself—reminders of corruption and dashed hopes, terror and crisis, that are borne around the globe by the increasingly powerful and centralized institutions of communication and mass media. His words arrive before us with the rest of our mediated reality and are presented for our reception or rejection.

Nguyen Ngoc Hung's moving testament was emptied into the general cultural pool one Sunday evening in the early spring of 1989, sandwiched between cola and cheeseburger commercials and rounded off with an Andy Rooney skit. The overall tone of this *60 Minutes'* report from present-day Vietnam, its unspoken yet unmistakable ideological drift, implies that there were no victors in that war, only victims, theirs and ours, sharing the effects and the pain in equal measure. Despite the absolute absurdity of such a notion, that kind of thinking represents a relatively commonplace understanding of where things now stand with the Vietnam War. Consequently, to think otherwise, as with most attempts to assert a different set of principles in the face of recently acquired ideological certainties, is accompanied by a sense of having offended against polite society. But then, that is how it is with ideologies that have come to be accepted as "natural," that have embedded themselves in public discourse as "common sense."

If it were true that the United States and Vietnam were equal victims of the war, then the populations of Los Angeles and New York would have been wiped out and those cities would have been reduced to ruins. Not only would major sections of the farming and industrial areas be, respectively, poisoned and destroyed, but the United States would also be isolated from world trade and international affairs. And the long-term toxic effects of such defoliants as Agent Orange would not be a matter of isolated tragedies reserved for veterans and their families, but would be a significant and debilitating factor among the general population.

So where do such notions that "there were no victors, only

victims" come from? How do they gain purchase in culture? Nguyen Ngoc Hung does not propose that the war can be understood in terms of an equality of suffering. Yet somewhere between the experience of the war and the process of its historical reception, an ideological twist is given his and other examples of Vietnam War memories. And it is not just the war that is being ideologically packaged for present-day mass consumption. The entire crisis-ridden decade of the 1960s, with its escalating cycles of domestic political activism and confrontation, is also being repackaged along the lines of a decidedly conservative ideological bias. Thus we begin with a war and we end with the ideological policing of a cultural and political crisis. This is not, of course, a crisis in its original 1960s "structure of feeling" (that emotional, psychological, and political milieu that temporarily—at the very least—ruptured an entire ideological order), but it is a crisis nonetheless, and one that continues to haunt a cultural imaginary that still cannot quite come to terms with the debacle of the Vietnam War.

The ruination wrought by the war, along with the continuing sense of trauma, anger, and cynicism, remains irrevocably embedded in American history and culture. Somewhere within the layers of accumulated rationalizing and media romanticizing, the terrible actualities linger—unbearable yet enduring, unacceptable yet unforgettable. The "real war" in Vietnam, replete with its "hideous secrets," as Michael Herr insists in *Dispatches*, was always in danger of becoming a hidden history in spite of (or perhaps because of) the miles of film and hours of television devoted to the war as it was taking place. Nevertheless, for those whom the war touched there will always be the "afterimage," the "dripping, laughing death-face [that] hid there in the newspapers and magazines and held to your television screens for hours after the set was turned off for the night."[1]

It is this "afterimage" that I explore in *Receptions of War*, the writing of which has involved a search for an appropriate framework that might allow access into that "imaginary zone" that culture creates "for what it excludes."[2] That search is one way of approaching the work that culture does, how it selects, appropriates, and banishes in a process that aims to smooth over problems and straighten out contradictions. Thus the term *culture*, along with the complex, always ideological work that cultural processes perform in media-saturated societies such as the United States, constitutes the often explicit, always implicit, organizing motivation for this study.

I should emphasize at the outset that *Receptions of War* is not intended as an encyclopedic survey of Vietnam War literature, television, or film. Rather, it outlines an approach to the study of modern American culture in an effort to draw connections between seemingly disparate historical themes and contemporary issues. It is not, I should further add, simply a study of the social production and consumption of texts, but also an attempt to grasp something of the nature of the cultural terrain within which the connections between writing and reading, filmmaking and viewing, are mediated. What I have tried to keep in mind throughout the writing and rewriting of this book is that, to borrow from Fredric Jameson, "everything is mediated by culture, to the point where even the political and the ideological levels have initially to be disentangled from their primary mode of representation, which is culture."[3]

As I suggested earlier, the writing of this book has not been easy, and it has taken much longer to complete than its length might suggest. In fact, it is quite a different book from the one that was beginning to take shape at the commencement of the 1980s, and the reasons for its transformation are easy to describe in broad outline. Since the late 1970s the Vietnam War has been the subject of an intense process of revisionism—a revisionism that has taken place at every level of American culture. Much of the literature and many of the films that began to appear in the middle to late 1970s seemed to be inaugurating a period of critical reassessment not only of the war itself but, more crucially, of the cultural determinants of subjectivity and political discourse that made war possible in the first place. That moment of critical examination turned out to be rather brief, however. In retrospect, it is now clear that the cultural and political shifts that were taking place in the period between the fall of Saigon in 1975 and the rise of Reaganism in 1980 represented an emergent sensibility of forces that inaugurated a return to a conservative hegemonic order. Once in place, political rhetoric began to turn again on the simplistic dichotomies of renewed Cold War thinking, within which the Vietnam War quite quickly became reinstated as a "noble cause." Thus, as one observer has written, "barely six years after the war in Vietnam had been brought to a painful and unsatisfying end, most of the fundamental ideological and symbolic preconditions that had brought it into being were back again."[4] Under those preconditions, critical reassessments of the war in popular culture tended to fade into the background. At the same time, neoconservative interpretations of Vietnam worked to transfer responsibility for the lost war from those who had planned and executed it to those who had opposed it.

Receptions of War, then, is concerned with illuminating the process through which an unpopular war has come to be received in popular culture. The organizational and theoretical focus of this book seeks to intervene in and, I hope, to advance what has become an increasingly crowded field of study. Many aspects of the Vietnam War in American culture are not fully developed here, in part because they have been adequately considered elsewhere.[5] Although I do consider at some length the crucial cultural determinants of gender and sexuality as central to our understanding of Vietnam War representations, for example, I have been mindful not to overlap with Susan Jeffords's excellent study *The Remasculinization of America.* Similarly, both Philip Beidler's *American Literature and the Experience of Vietnam* and John Hellmann's *American Myth and the Legacy of Vietnam* offer insights into the ways in which the Vietnam War challenged time-honored national myths and cultural symbols;[6] in *Receptions of War,* however, I take a different approach by exploring how certain myths and symbols gain currency in culture, how they structure what are essentially ideological and political perceptions and subjectivities, and finally, how they have been deconstructed and reconstructed over a twenty-year process of revision.

The first chapter of *Receptions of War* analyzes what I call the "Vietnam continuum" in American popular culture. The purpose of the chapter is twofold. It aims, first, to suggest the breadth of the social and political crisis that the Vietnam War continues to generate in American culture, and second, to forward a number of theoretical approaches by means of which we might better understand the ideological nature of contemporary thinking about Vietnam. The investigation of "culture" becomes the more specific subject of chapter 2. Here, after exploring the historically divergent approaches offered by American studies and British cultural studies, I propose a "critical paradigm" that views culture not just in its anthropological sense, as a whole way of life, but as an arena where the ongoing struggle to assert hegemonic imperatives and meanings takes place. Drawing upon the theoretical issues raised in the first two chapters, chapter 3 analyzes a selection of intellectual and popular responses to the Vietnam War. Here I consider the historical and cultural processes within and against which intellectuals and popular novelists and memoirists (veterans for the most part) have struggled to comprehend the nature of the Vietnam catastrophe. The point of this chapter is not to survey the entire output of Vietnam War writing but to reconsider some of the major critical acts and themes that continue to pervade political discourse and popular memory. Moving from written to visual texts, chapter 4 situates the films of the Vietnam War within the contested history of their production and consumption. Although excesses of visual style and narrative structure appear early in the history of Vietnam War films (particularly in relation to the figuration of the male body), melodrama came into its own as perhaps the dominant representational mode in the mid-1980s with the success of *Platoon* and the appearance of such television series as *China Beach*. That rise to dominance is the focus of the fifth and final chapter, which analyzes Vietnam War representations in terms of their melodramatic affects and effects.

Thus, across the various chapters and through close analysis of individual texts, *Receptions of War* traces some of the twists and turns in the continuous and always unequal struggle to disorganize and reorganize the meaning of the Vietnam War in American culture. I take this struggle over recent history and popular memory to be axiomatic of the ways in which hegemonic formations attempt to articulate, appropriate, and repress those emergent sensibilities that offer, or might come to offer, a challenge to the (always temporary) order of things. The Vietnam War lingers on in American culture as a reminder of the vulnerability of hegemonic formations, and of how quickly the seemingly legitimate perspectives of the powerful can be exposed as violently corrupt and self-interested.

RECEPTIONS OF WAR

THE VIETNAM CONTINUUM

It's back! Napalm, fire fights, body bags, Hueys,
rice paddies, Victor Charlie, search-and-destroy,
the quagmire, the living room war. After 16 years,
the Vietnam War returns to American television.
This time, it's playing prime time, and the enemy
is Bill Cosby.

PETER BOYER, "IS IT PRIME TIME FOR VIETNAM?"

THE Vietnam War has indeed returned to the
American popular cultural scene, only this time, as the above
quotation from the *New York Times* (2 August 1987) makes
clear, it has returned with a vengeance. Following in the wake
of the immensely popular film *Platoon* (1985), the CBS television series *Tour of Duty*, which first aired in the fall of 1987,
brought images of men at war in Vietnam back to the American home on a weekly basis. In a return of a similar kind,
ABC launched its Vietnam series *China Beach* in the spring
of 1988. That program, with its emphasis on women at war,
complicated the conventional view of the Vietnam War, situ-
ating a parallel drama of women's relationships and everyday life alongside the drama of combat and men at war.
Despite the hesitation surrounding the initial release of
Vietnam TV dramas (television executives feared that any
attempt at either "serious" or "light" treatment of the Vietnam War would alienate audiences), those series managed to

survive three and four seasons as well as shifts in format and changes in time slots, thus offering a challenge not only to *The Cosby Show* but also to the entire range of prime-time family entertainment.

There is, of course, a good deal of irony intended in the use of the above quotation on the reception of *Tour of Duty.* For when a networks "ratings war" becomes synonymous with the "war at home" it would appear that we have moved well beyond what was once considered a legitimate realm of cul- ture and politics and into a realm of the simulacrum. And while the issue today is no longer the "living room war" in quite the sense of that term as it emerged in the late 1960s, in many ways the Vietnam War continues to collapse distinc- tions between domestic and foreign policy, private and pub- lic spheres. In a profound way, the Vietnam War constitutes what Michel Foucault would call "a node within a network of discourses," the site of a struggle over popular memory and cultural meaning.[1] It is in this sense that we can say that the Vietnam War was never a punctual or singular event, just as it was never confined to a single mode of representation. For this reason I take a broad, interdisciplinary approach to the topic of Vietnam and its various representations in an effort to explore the highly fraught terrain of American culture that was brought into sharp focus in the 1960s, and that remains profoundly contested within contemporary experience.

The vocal debates in the 1980s concerning U.S. policy in Central America, along with the troubled and eventually il- legal attempts by the Reagan administration to obtain mili- tary aid for Contra operations in Nicaragua, represented, among other things, a powerful demonstration of at least one set of the continuing effects of the contested status of the Vietnam War in American culture. In spite of quite dramatic attempts to raise the specter of a rampant communism on America's doorstep—a strategy that regularly deployed the rhetoric of the "high" Cold War of the 1950s, not to mention a rather tired version of the domino theory ("If Nicaragua should fall . . .")—a congressional majority remained skep- tical, the American public was for the most part suspicious,

and a fairly widespread peace movement managed to organized around the issue. Even in 1991, after the victory of the
American-led coalition forces in Kuwait, it still remained
necessary for the popular press to proclaim that America had
finally triumphed over the psychic traumas of Vietnam. Indeed, even before the fighting in the Persian Gulf began,
President George Bush was driven to proclaim that "this will
not be another Vietnam." Responding to Bush's words, journalists turned out dozens of articles designed to demonstrate
the crucial differences between the two conflicts—the technological advances since Vietnam, the different topographies of
the two regions, the cultural differences between the two enemies, and so forth. Some of those articles were accompanied
by photographs of American troops in Vietnam ("frightened
draftees"), which were juxtaposed with images of the "all-
volunteer" troops in Saudi Arabia ("superb motivation").[2]

Far from being over, and despite elaborate claims to the
contrary, the Vietnam War has maintained a stranglehold on
the American imagination, so much so that presidents must
acknowledge and negotiate the memory of Vietnam as a first
order of business before involving the country in armed conflict. In short, the skepticism and cynicism that Vietnam generated in American culture has still to be factored into the
management of military operations and into the political
rhetoric aimed at garnering public consent.

This skepticism, this distrust of military solutions for Third
World problems, was recognized as such a regular feature of
the contemporary political process that it became designated
as the "Vietnam syndrome." Depending on the point of view,
the term means, on the one hand, the welcome continuation
of the anti–Vietnam War sensibility, with its insistence on
diplomatic responses to world events that are based on "realistic" assessments and, above all, on moral evaluations. On
the other hand, the Vietnam syndrome has been viewed as
an unacceptable restraint on covert operations and military
interventions, which are seen by many conservatives as legitimate instruments of diplomacy and foreign policy. Thus
the term has not only been made to signify contradictory

positions but has also become symbolically loaded: it is at once a coded referent to certain atavistic, or militaristic, tendencies that must be guarded against in the name of rational and moral relations with other countries; and at the same time it is a term marking a sickness or weakness for which a cure is needed so that a more strident and unfettered foreign policy may once again emerge.[3]

What the 1980s demonstrated was that the latter had indeed emerged, but that the "cure" was far from complete. Even after years of campaigning on behalf of a military solution to the "Sandinista problem," the Reagan administration remained unable to supply the Contras legally. Like Richard Nixon before him, Ronald Reagan resorted to extraparliamentary procedures and methods, which would eventually lead to the "Irangate" scandal. (It is interesting to note, in relation to what I am calling the Vietnam continuum, that many of the individuals involved in the Iran-Contra affair were veterans of covert operations conducted during the Vietnam War. The exception was Oliver North, a combat veteran, who went on to garner perhaps the most notoriety and the added distinction of a television docudrama dedicated to his rise and fall.) Political discourse, however, constitutes only one part of the Vietnam continuum, albeit a particularly visible and troubling one. Indeed, the conflicts at the political level are manifestations of a much deeper cultural operation that has been at work over the past twenty years, and this operation has itself been in conflict over the meaning of the Vietnam War in American life.

In an essay that explores these issues, John Carlos Rowe claims that the war "remains radically ambiguous, undecidable, and indeterminate to the American public." The sheer range and heterogeneity of materials that now cluster around the somewhat unstable signifier *Vietnam*, he argues, "seems to grow even more explicit and tangled with every new effort to 'heal' the wounds, every new monument and parade, movie and book."[4] In line with this view is my argument that the Vietnam War has been detached from history and absorbed into American culture as a "discursive process" in which meaning results from the often antagonistic conjuncture of propositions, expressions, and representations. In other words, discourse and meaning are constructed in a process of protracted struggle and negotiation among contending political factions, cultural systems of representation, social groups, and their historically lived experiences. Thus the most crucial terms can change their meaning depending upon the positions from which they are articulated and the contexts in which they are received.

In this way, words, images, expressions, and even colloquial speech (the authenticating stock-in-trade of the Vietnam novel and film) find their meanings—however temporary and unstable—through reference to the cultural conditions and material practices from which and within which they are inscribed ideologically. Generally, the positions from which we receive the signs of a discursive process are institutional, embracing the realms of media, education, religion, politics, the military, and so forth. Therefore, the position and institutional setting will together determine what can and cannot be said in relation to particular discourses.[5] That is not to imply that discourses are closed systems, any more than individual subjects are the product of a single discourse. For just as it is possible to talk about interdiscursive play within discursive formations, so, too, is subjectivity "the product of the effects of discursive practices traversing the subject throughout its history."[6]

Although the discursive status of the war is central to this study, I nevertheless insist throughout on the need to attend to historical conditions, material effects, and political and economic forces. Power and its consequences are never simply discursive, and it would be a mistake to think that the terrorizing events that "scar human bodies," such as poverty, racism, sexism, and war, can be fully understood through recourse to linguistic models alone. As much as the old Marxist base-superstructure model no longer offers an entirely compelling explanation of contemporary society, it still remains necessary to preserve, as Cornel West has argued, "a measure of synecdochical thinking, thinking that would still invoke relations of parts to the whole."[7] As I demonstrate in subsequent chapters, discursive formations in fact work to limit and contain desire and knowledge within a relatively narrow range of possibilities, and do so within the context of historically specific structures of power and production. In the early 1960s, for example, the possibility that the government was lying, or that the Vietnam War could be anything but an honorable cause, was unthinkable to most people—such possibilities were simply not yet on the linguistic or cultural radar. That the experience of the Vietnam War taught many people otherwise, forcing them beyond the boundaries of established discourses, accounts in good part for their subsequent alienation from American society and for the silence that surrounded the veterans' experience of American culture for many years afterward. Their critical knowledge of the Vietnam War represented a countermemory not only to official accounts but also to the "sanitized" and "romanticized" discourse of all wars.[8]

The extravagant claims of some postmodernisms, which announce the end of history, the end of ideology, and the final leveling of culture "with no regrets for the past and no more borders to cross,"[9] fail to account for this fundamental complexity of texts, subjects, and contexts. If everything is a shimmering surface without depth, where history, experience, and the commodity finally blend, then there would be, for example, no dispute between CBS and General William C. Westmoreland over the latter's account of his conduct of the war in Vietnam. There would be, in other words, no struggle, no contested meanings, no essential difference between war and war films.

Certainly, any analysis of discursive formations and the Vietnam War must account for an ever more complex and antagonistic knot of contradictions. Myths of an undefeated American military, for instance, coexist with the fact of a lost war, just as certain kinds of political rhetoric that attempt to establish the Vietnam War as a "noble cause" jostle for ascendancy with historical accounts, memoirs, and such leaked revelations as the Pentagon Papers. Similarly, a culturally and politically valorized tradition of combat heroism has been forced to adjust itself to the heroism of refusal, just as novels of patriotic celebration now sit side by side with novels of political condemnation. Furthermore, Vietnam veterans have been variously positioned as crybabies, dutiful sons, dangerous misfits, or patriotic warriors. Of course, none of these categories are internally pure; that is, they are not without their own contradictions and elisions. In addition, those who encounter these texts and discourses do so in social settings where other texts and discourses, other affiliations and practices, are constantly at work. Given the pervasive distrust of political leaders, military apologists, and professional commentators that set in with a vengeance during the Vietnam War, and given the existence of what Foucault calls the countermemory of historical experience, a good deal of the war's cultural discourses remain contested and ambiguous because they represent decisive stakes in an as-yet-undecided battle. As with everything else, there is a history to that battle.

As we move into the closing years of the century it is perhaps easy to forget that American culture was not always so saturated with the reified commercial spectacles of Vietnam that are now such a pervasive part of the nation's mass-produced popular culture. What we can identify in pre-Vietnam American culture, however, are the ideological components and political preconditions that would eventually prepare the way for war in Vietnam. Perhaps more to the point, by the 1950s a majority of American living rooms were equipped with television sets. In an era marked by a powerful convergence of technological possibilities and ideological fundamentalism, television quickly became the main cultural conduit through which the political concepts of the Cold War were articulated and naturalized. Indeed, as J. Fred MacDonald has shown, the "video road to Vietnam" gradually took shape in the decidedly propagandistic, Cold War slant given to both entertainment and news programming in the 1950s, which, although rarely concerned specifically with Vietnam, prepared Americans for military interventions in the internal affairs of other nations.[10]

One of the effects of this new representational technology in American culture was the supplementing of the residual and still variously active ideology of "isolationism" with the new ideology of "containment." That shift in the politics of American culture marks one of the major elements of the post–World War II "settlement," a historical formation that brought together dominant sections of capital and labor, along with influential groupings of politicians, intellectuals, and military leaders. That emergent formation would eventually reach its zenith with John F. Kennedy's "Camelot" and its apocalypse with Vietnam and Watergate.

By the mid-1960s the ideological absolutes of global politics promoted by television culture in the 1950s gave way to the so-called television war, making it impossible to ignore the immediacy of the images that flowed from Vietnam on a daily basis—or to miss the images of social confrontation and disintegration that the war inexorably quickened at home. And then, seemingly just as suddenly, the flow of television images from Vietnam came to a halt in the early 1970s and a stifling silence followed (*The Big Chill*) as political leaders and cultural tastemakers attempted to guide national attention elsewhere.

Commenting on this development, Peter Marin has described a "cultural paralysis" that set in as the American people turned away from the difficult issues raised by the Vietnam War in the 1970s. "What paralyzed us," Marin writes, "was not simply the guilt felt about Vietnam, but our inability to confront and comprehend that guilt: our refusal to face squarely what happened and why, and our unwillingness to determine in the light of the past our moral obligations for the future." Marin locates part of the blame for this cultural malaise within the Vietnam War literature itself. In his view, that literature is "the work of distraught and alienated men who are unable to locate any sort of vision or binding values." Furthermore, he argues, those authors are too caught up in the American system of myth, and are therefore unwilling "to confront directly the realities of the war, or to have considered it at least in part from the Vietnamese point of view . . . in terms of their suffering rather than ours."[11]

The indignant and morally disturbed tone of Marin's article is fairly common among many liberal-left intellectuals who contemplate post-Vietnam America. And although Marin's position is a welcome corrective to the discourse of remilitarization that came to dominate American culture in the 1980s, its assumption of a straightforward and unmediated relationship between authorship and popular reception remains unable to account for the ways in which meaning is produced, appropriated, and distributed across the uneven hierarchies of textual consumption. Moreover, Marin gives us no sense of the manner in which images and information about the war have shaped and are shaped by the institutions of education, information, and mass communication. More crucially, the assumption informing his view is one that envisions a kind of democratic marketplace in which texts are consumed on the basis of an ideologically neutral form of equal opportunity.

That conventional view of how texts enter public discourse is one that misses the fundamentally conflicted nature of textual production and consumption. As Jim Collins argues in *Uncommon Cultures*, texts no longer "fulfill specific co-ordinated functions in some kind of master system." Rather, texts enter a fragmented cultural arena in which they must struggle to "clear a space for themselves within specific semiotic environments." The intensity of that struggle in the present (which Collins views as not only fragmented but also decentered) has become "increasingly complicated due to competition among different discourses for the same status, for fulfilling the same or similar functions for a given culture."[12] In a sense, then, Vietnam War texts had to displace the texts of other American wars in order to establish a recognizable semiotic status, or popular function, for themselves. That process was particularly intense in the 1970s because of a general and lingering distaste for the Vietnam War that influenced publishers and readers alike. By the late 1970s, however, a number of Vietnam texts had become best-sellers, and a few, like Tim O'Brien's *Going after Cacciato*, had won literary prizes. But in the process of having cleared a cultural and semiotic space for themselves, these Vietnam texts had irrevocably altered the status and function of previous war stories.

As Paul Fussell points out, it is now impossible to view World War II without seeing it through "the prism of the Vietnam War." A vigorously controlled journalistic censorship during World War II guaranteed the elevation of a romantic and sentimental picture of wartime realities. The same propagandistic manipulations "might have sweetened the actualities of Vietnam," Fussell observes, "if television and a vigorous uncensored moral journalism hadn't been brought to bear."[13] In good part, then, the more immediate ways in which the Vietnam War was reported back to America, and the accessibility of the images of the effects of war, changed public perceptions of war in general. In this way, the displacing power of Vietnam War texts stems in part from their position within the intertextual system of images, narratives, and political discourses that became embedded in American culture during the 1960s. Thus, as Edward Said insists, "all texts essentially dislodge other texts or, more frequently, take the place of something else."[14]

The appearance of Graham Greene's *The Quiet American* in 1955 provides an important example in support of Said's proposition and at the same time illuminates the processes of reception and displacement that have formed around the Vietnam War. Greene's novel also fulfills Marin's demand that intellectuals engage with the moral questions raised by the Vietnam War within the context of both Vietnamese and American sensibilities. But in point of fact, *The Quiet American* was attacked by American critics and failed to find a popular audience at the time of its initial reception. Now, however, it is cited not only as a classic example of Vietnam War writing but also as a prophetic exposition of ideologically flawed national discourses on global politics.

Despite Greene's insistence that *The Quiet American* "is a

story and not a piece of history," the novel was nevertheless inspired by events that Greene witnessed as a reporter in Vietnam during the early 1950s. In those years the French colonial army, which was heavily subsidized by the United States, was engaged in a last-ditch effort to defeat Ho Chi Minh's guerrilla forces. In 1954, however, the French were decisively defeated in the battle of Dien Bien Phu, and America began to take a much more visible and active role in Vietnamese affairs. This included massive aid programs, military training and advisory programs, and covert manipulations of the internal political affairs of Vietnam. All of these efforts quickly solidified behind the figure of Ngo Dinh Diem, a Catholic mandarin in a predominately Buddhist country, who ruled South Vietnam from 1954 until his assassination during the American-supported coup d'état of 1963. The early 1950s was, then, a crucial period in the history of American involvement in Vietnam, and Greene bore witness to the ideological and rhetorical shifts that took place as the French colonial war against Vietnamese nationalism gave way to the American crusade against communism. Thus, on the heels of the French defeat, Vietnam shifted rapidly to the center of American Cold War strategies and quickly became a vital test case of American resolve in a global policy of containing communism.

What *The Quiet American* reveals, in the figure of Alden Pyle, a State Department agent, is a particularly American male subjectivity that has been narrowly structured by Cold War global strategies and obsessions. Alden Pyle lives in a world of clichés and speaks a language that has become not only abstracted from the objects it seeks to describe but also detached from the moral obligation to take responsibility for the results of one's personal actions. In this sense, Pyle prefigures a whole history of what the Vietnam War journalist Michael Herr calls "Vietnam news-speak"—an official Orwellian jargon that characterized the news coming from Vietnam and that was, to quote Herr again, "of such delicate locutions that it's often impossible to know even remotely the thing being described."[15] In *The Quiet American* Greene describes a similar discursive jargon at the operative center of the "American mission" during the 1950s. The novel's narrator, a British journalist called Thomas Fowler, says of Pyle that he "never saw anything he hadn't heard in a lecture hall, and his writers and lecturers made a fool of him. When he saw a dead body he couldn't even see the wounds. A Red menace, a soldier of democracy." Moreover, Pyle "was as incapable of imagining pain or danger to himself as he was incapable of conceiving the pain he might cause others." He was, as Greene puts it, "impregnably armoured by his good intentions and his ignorance."[16]

Greene's representation of a fragmented language and subjectivity pleased neither the American critics nor the American reading public. That displeasure led to an attempt to rewrite Greene's version of American foreign policy in Vietnam, and to refashion the mentality that supported American interests abroad. In 1958 William Lederer and Eugene Burdick presented the American public with a different vision of American involvement in Southeast Asia in their novel *The Ugly American*—a novel that hardly conceals its reworking of Greene's initial premises.[17] Here, a number of "fictional" characters (including one Edwin B. Hillandale, based, as was Green's Alden Pyle, on the real-life figure of Edward G. Lansdale) are celebrated in terms of a new form of frontier heroism—a heroism contrasted with the ugly and usually obese career diplomats who huddle in the embassies, enjoying lavish life-styles, hobnobbing with the colonial elites. The "real" Americans—those like Pyle and Hillandale, that is—are determined to combat such elitism and to move quickly out among the villages in order to confront Communist subversion on its own turf. It is assumed that such services on behalf of an anti-Communist foreign policy and in the name of "democracy" and "freedom" will automatically be appreciated by the embattled peasantry.

Interestingly enough, the Hollywood film adaptation of *The Quiet American* (also released in 1958) reverses Greene's order of things and substitutes Lederer and Burdick's instead. Here, Alden Pyle is portrayed as a heroic and idealist American hero with none of Greene's criticisms or equivocations. In Greene's novel, Pyle supplies arms and explosives to one of Vietnam's most violent and antidemocratic factions. Following a street bombing, in which many civilians are killed and maimed by explosives supplied by Pyle, the British journalist Thomas Fowler is driven to intervene against Pyle. This intervention eventually costs Pyle his life. But what Greene is at pains to demonstrate is the sense of moral outrage that motivates Fowler's actions. And what he also makes clear is the amoral behavior of those like Pyle who cause untold misery in the name of Cold War abstractions. In the film version, however, Pyle is characterized as an altruistic importer of children's toys for Vietnamese orphans, and Fowler, now singularly motivated by jealously, becomes the despised villain of the piece and the murderer of Pyle.

In this way, *The Ugly American* and the Hollywood adaptation of *The Quiet American* substitute populism and racial harmony for Greene's critique of American imperialism and racial tension. Not surprisingly, *The Ugly American* was a best-seller. Senator John F. Kennedy was so impressed by it that he distributed copies to every U.S. senator. In 1960 the novel became a theme in the American presidential election between Kennedy and Richard Nixon, the heir to Dwight D. Eisenhower's political legacy.[18] Thus, given the powerful media amplification of *The Ugly American*'s themes—and given the still-fresh memory of an indecisive Korean War and the powerful discourses of the Cold War, with its show trials, witchhunts, and blacklisting, not to mention the demonic portrayal of the Soviet Union as seemingly ahead in the space race—Americans were unable to understand or receive the critical picture that Greene provided of American "innocence" running amok in Southeast Asia. Lederer and Burdick's version of the Pyle syndrome was pitched to the correct cultural wavelength, and under President Kennedy's stewardship that syndrome would shift almost seamlessly to such counterinsurgency symbols as the Green Berets and the more benign, although nonetheless ideological, interventions of the Peace Corps. Given these cultural circumstances it is not surprising that Greene's novel failed to find an audience, since his rendering of the historical, political, and cultural complexities of Vietnam, and of America's intervention there, was inaccessible to many Americans in the 1950s. *The Quiet American* would have to wait until the early 1970s, when the Vietnam War had forcibly reconfigured the ideological coordinates of public consciousness and had cleared a discursive space in which the dangerous banality of Alden Pyle could be recognized.

The inability of Americans to receive a critical version of U.S. involvement in Vietnam has led the journalist and novelist David Halberstam to speculate about conditions of popular reception in the 1960s. Specifically, Halberstam is concerned to explain the failure of his Vietnam War novel *One Very Hot Day* (1968) and the consequent success of that same novel in the mid-1980s. During the turbulent 1960s, Halberstam contends, no one wanted to read a novel about combat in Vietnam because, as he puts it, "television's coverage of the war . . . with its startling immediacy (it was, after all, the living room war) had at least temporarily eclipsed the need for fiction."[19]

On the surface, here would seem to be a cogent and, by now, a familiar analysis: the American people were inundated with images of the Vietnam War from their TV sets; they (and not the Vietnamese) were the ones who were "bombarded" by the war on a daily basis. As the television critic Michael Arlen has written, Vietnam colored everything on television in the late 1960s, and under these conditions, one could well sympathize with Halberstam's claim that people were sick of Vietnam and in no mood for the kind of fictional distance provided by novelists.[20]

And yet, one might ask, for whom was fiction eclipsed? Certainly it was not eclipsed for the large section of the popular reading public that made Roger Moore's *The Green Berets* a best-seller in 1966. Moreover, Halberstam seems to apply dubious notions about what constitutes documentary and fiction to his understanding of Vietnam and television, as though the one form was immediate and the other mediated. But that, in fact, is a false distinction. American depictions of Vietnam have always been highly mediated, and the line separating document from fiction, and experience from representation, has always been in some way transgressed.

A brief sketch of the history of television's shifting representations of the Cold War in Asia will suffice to demonstrate that mediational paradigms have always marked the world according to television. Between the late 1940s and the very early 1960s, most of the television images of Southeast Asia were supplied by foreign television companies and by various American government agencies. American news stories tended to be structured by the *Quiet American/Ugly American* debate. For example, in the late 1950s ABC sponsored a program entitled "The Splendid American," a documentary that told the story of Tom Dooley (pictured as an idealistic Alden Pyle type), who was reported as doing "good works" among the Asian natives. Between 1961 and 1967, the years between Kennedy's commitment of a few thousand combat advisors and Lyndon Johnson's escalation of the war, the media began further to construct Vietnam as "an American story." And as the war escalated into a full-scale conflict, it became as much a televised war as a television war. In popular terms, it was "the living room war," the first war to be televised daily to the American public.

In the early 1960s television tended to represent the war through uncoordinated messages clustered around familiar ideological signifiers, such as the domino theory. By the mid-1960s, however, narrative patterns were clearly emerging. One such pattern, based on a unifying plot device that one critic calls "who is the enemy," took its structure from daily measurements of enemy casualties. Following the Tet Offensive of 1968, however, it began to be generally conceded on television news broadcasts that the war had reached a stalemate. Consequently, the nighttime news now shifted its focus away from stories of American combat to what one ABC news executive referred to as stories based on the premise that "we are on our way out of Vietnam."[21]

Gradually, the Vietnam War became a Vietnamese story.

Vietnam was represented as a place of doubts and uncertain-
ties (as indeed Greene had suggested previously), and not as
a new frontier for the reenactment of the American spirit, as
Lederer and Burdick had claimed. Then with the fall of Saigon
in 1975, President Gerald Ford and Henry Kissinger, among
others, advised the American people to put the Vietnam experience behind them. With the fall of Saigon the Vietnam
War was, so to speak, to constitute a closed chapter on a
problem no longer in need of narration but rather one best
repressed and forgotten.

From this brief description it is clear that the Vietnam War
itself was not the only problem. It was what the war inspired
within American culture that was—and is—the problem. With
the exception of a handful of critical documentaries, the war
is not represented as the result of political, intellectual, and
cultural miscalculation. It continues to mark instead the site
of domestic upheaval and confrontation, as it also signifies a
crisis or break in the structural components of the post–World
War II ideological formation. This crisis, as John Hellmann
claims, has sunk deep roots into the symbolic and mythic
bedrock of American culture. "Americans entered Vietnam,"
writes Hellmann,

with certain expectations that a story, a distinctly American story,
would unfold. When the story of America in Vietnam turned into
something unexpected, the true nature of the larger story of America itself became the subject of intense cultural dispute. On the
deepest level, the legacy of Vietnam is the disruption of our story,
of our explanation of the past and vision of the future.[22]

Hellmann further claims that, at least historically, the United
States has been relatively free of outside interference and thus
able to develop its resources and institutions by the light of
its own internal dynamic. Hence, America has never been
forced to confront "its guilts and flaws." The cultural dispute
engendered by the war in Vietnam, however, brought into
question the most fundamental assumptions through which
Americans engaged with the world. One of the lasting results

has been a fragmenting of the sedimented layers of American mythology. Thus, as novelists, filmmakers, and television producers attempted to reconstruct the experience of Vietnam in terms of a new mythic heroism, they touched on a fundamental contradiction between the accumulated currency of established myths, which are still actively available in the video archives of popular culture, and the emergent contingencies of entertainment and ideology.

The Vietnam War era, then, was a period when the inner workings of social institutions and cultural values were made starkly visible and exposed to critical inspection. It remains a period in American history that continues to haunt the political culture of the nation as well as its popular memory and imagination. Of course, it can be argued that in all historical periods there exist dynamic tensions between what Raymond Williams describes as "the official consciousness of epoch—codified in its doctrines and legislation—and the whole process of actually living its consequences."[23] But at the time of the Vietnam War that process was intensified to the point where large sections of the population were forced by the nature of events from what Williams calls "lived ideology" into "critical knowledge." The myths and ideologies that had been forged in the Cold War no longer provided reliable guides to, or were entirely capable of mediating the contradictions within, the actual world of lived experience.

Vietnam altered many of the fundamental coordinates of American society and culture, just as it undermined the economy and poisoned national politics. And in the face of the almost unimaginable scale of Vietnamese civilian deaths (calculated by Robert McNamara as one thousand per week from aerial bombing alone) and the creation of an estimated four million refugees (approximately one quarter of the population),[24] many Americans came to feel a deep-seated sense of disgust at what their government and the military were doing in Vietnam. Even McNamara, who had done so much to set the war in motion, came to feel ashamed of America's way of war in Vietnam. In a memorandum to Johnson in 1967, McNamara wrote that the "picture of the world's great-

est superpower killing or seriously injuring 1,000 noncomba-
tants a week, while trying to pound a tiny backward nation
into submission on an issue whose merits are hotly dis-
puted, is not a pretty one."[25] But perhaps one of the most
intuitive expressions of this emergent sense of the historical
rupture caused by the war came from Carl Oglesby, one of
the leaders of the Students for a Democratic Society: "We can
scarcely return unchanged from this spectacle to dream the
old dreams, take comfort in the old verities . . . with this war,
history becomes the intimate affair of each of us, a private act
for which each of us has to account personally."[26]

In recent times we have witnessed a reemergence of the
term *living room war* (which was initially used to describe
television's coverage of the war in the 1960s) as a familiar
metaphor for the more general relationship between the war
in Vietnam and its representation in literature, film, and television. It is also a term that misses much of the meaning of
this relationship. Indeed, *living room war* is now often used
to reconstruct the influence of television from a conservative
or new-revisionist point of view. From this perspective it is
argued that television and popular journalism undermined
the war effort at home with a consistent flow of negative
images and stories that stressed the violence of the war
rather than "the nobility of the mission" to stem the tide of
communism.

But the term *living room war* can certainly be interpreted
in another way, in a way that is consistently elided in the
attacks made by such New Right organizations as Accuracy
in Media. If the Vietnam War erupted into the domestic
space of the American home by means of television, that
space was already highly contested and in conflict. The
American family was already at war, as it were, and the
home became one of the crucial battlegrounds where an assumed tradition of stable cultural values wrestled in deadly
combat with the lived cultural forms of a postindustrial society. Here is the more pressing meaning of the living room
war, given that the living room in the late 1960s was no
longer the site of domestic bliss that it had been constructed

to be in the 1950s, but rather an arena of conflict that had become crisscrossed with an array of media interventions and compromised by the surveillance and paternalism of professional social agencies. The family had also become an arena where youth railed against the authority of parents, and where countercultural forms of behavior questioned traditional forms of gender, race, and class, marking the breakdown of lived ideology and the emergence of various kinds of critical knowledge. The living room war, then, signaled not the war in Vietnam so much as the war taking place at home.

Returning to Halberstam, we can now see how his claim that the war eclipsed the need for fiction highlights an important issue. What the television war had eclipsed was the desire not for fiction but for war itself, by making the romantic conventions of warfare untenable. In general terms, then, the fundamental question of Vietnam and representation remains a question of reception—of how the effects of the Vietnam War have constructed for some, and deconstructed for others, the subjectivity necessary for war. And here, it seems to me, is the site of a fundamental fracture or crisis in the post-Vietnam cultural process, a crisis that is being played out across the full range of popular entertainment forms.

The stakes in this process are viewed by many on the political right as crucial to the continuation of an American world profile that is "manly" and militarily willing to "accept any sacrifice." But for all the political rhetoric that accompanied the advent of Reaganism, with its sexualized metaphors of making America "stand tall" and able to "perform" once again as a proud and active global force, it is clear that the cultural-political discourse of war has been irrevocably altered by the Vietnam experience. John Kennedy was perhaps the last president who could draw unself-consciously upon the war mentality and the myth of the always righteous warrior leader. After Vietnam such confidence has always been in danger of being received as parody, masquerade, or satirical posturing. And that danger is yet another example of the accumulation of spectacle, a logjam of simulations borne back ceaselessly into the utopian past of a cultural imaginary.

This line of argument returns us, inevitably, to the present context of television and the battle of the networks. *Tour of Duty* faces *The Cosby Show* in the ratings war, and the media critics can agree that the "living room war" is finally back. It almost goes without saying that the emphasis on the family and on domestic space that so characterized television programming in the 1980s seems more indebted to the cultural imaginary of the 1950s. Indeed, the notions that circulated immediately during and after the Vietnam War—that family structures must be changed, that issues of gender, race, and class must be addressed and redressed—continue to serve as a subtext that barely conceals the failure to fundamentally restructure either the family or the marketplace in American culture. In other words, the tensions that have long accompanied the receptions of the Vietnam War in American life continue almost unabated today.

The most recent images and representations of Vietnam, then, confirm not so much that the war has returned to the American domestic scene, in the sense of that which was missing now being found, as that a new cycle of cultural mediations on the war has emerged. The danger to be avoided now is one of slipping into a kind of Nietzschean despondency in which that return is accepted as an inevitable return of the same. All moments of historical change, as the events of the 1960s so vividly demonstrate, do not simply offer opportunities for further reproductions and reaffirmations of hegemonic power and control. Such moments also present opportunities for opening up new forms of struggle, reconstruction, and interpretation.

The return of an unpopular war in the popular culture of the 1980s and 1990s suggests that just this kind of contested cultural operation is at work. For as much as the culture industries strive to popularize the Vietnam War, in the process they cannot avoid touching on the very issues that made the war a bitterly divisive and controversial event in the first place. Even the most stridently prowar texts cannot avoid

the uncomfortable fact that the most powerful, most tech-
nologically advanced Western nation could not force its political will upon a small Asian country. Vietnam could be destroyed—and in several meanings of the term, it was ruined—
but it could not be made over in the abstract images of another
culture's ideological agenda.

What I have tried to suggest with the survey set forth in
this chapter is that the war was a whole cultural event that
eventually drew into itself, and made strange, a whole way
of life that had come into existence in the aftermath of World
War II. That way of life, with all of its political assumptions,
intellectual conceits, social rituals, and cultural processes,
somehow unraveled during the 1960s, and what has been
taking place ever since is a contested process of restructuring
a new social compact. The crisis of authority let loose by the
upheavals of the 1960s and the Vietnam War has not made
for an easy transition from one power bloc to the next, as the
troubled administrations of Gerald Ford and Jimmy Carter
so clearly demonstrated. Too many pieces of unfinished
business from the 1960s continue to clutter the political
arena. Moreover, as I have tried to indicate, the new conservative hegemony that emerged with the spectacle of Reaganism in the 1980s could not completely displace the remnants of the older progressive sensibility, any more than it
could disperse or suppress the lingering activist tradition of
the 1960s.

To my mind, then, the 1980s were not simply about the
triumph of neoconservativism. Those years also witnessed a
period of cultural restructuring that turned, in large part, on
the hinge of the Vietnam War. In order to remilitarize the
culture, by which I mean the attempt to set in place the
essential semiotic and representational systems that make
war not only thinkable but, at some level, desirable, it has
been necessary to repossess the Vietnam War and to refur-
bish it along ideological lines more acceptable to the ruling
powers. It is this process of reclaiming and revising that I
explore in subsequent chapters. Before turning to Vietnam

texts specifically, however, I take a brief detour through the history and theory that informs my own approach to the study of contemporary culture in an effort to suggest the very conditions of possibility for this study. As I hope to show, the processes that made war possible in the 1960s had a profound impact on intellectual discourses and academic disciplines, which were forced to come to terms with the meaning and function of both an unpopular war and its links to an ever-expanding popular culture.

2

CONFORMITY, CONSENSUS, AND CULTURAL STUDIES

> There are in fact no masses; there are only ways of
> seeing people as masses. In an urban industrial soci-
> ety there are many opportunities for such ways of
> seeing. The point is not to reiterate the objective
> conditions but to consider, personally and collec-
> tively, what these have done to our thinking. The
> fact is, surely, that a way of seeing other people
> which has become characteristic of our kind of
> society, has been capitalised for the purpose of
> political or cultural exploitation.
>
> RAYMOND WILLIAMS, *CULTURE AND SOCIETY, 1780–1950*

IN ITS merely interdisciplinary formation in the
academy, what now passes for cultural studies often rests
secure on an optimistic approach to popular culture that
plays a watered-down populism against, most typically, earlier, more pessimistic and elitist, models of culture. Thus,
against the view of mass culture that assumed a politically
manipulated or passive mass audience, the consumer of popular culture is now often celebrated as a rascally independent decoder of texts, forever spinning off his or her indi-
vidualized forms of resistant readings. Although claiming to
speak in the name of the people and thus of politics, this

25

newer, more affirmative view of popular culture ultimately jettisons any notion of politics, at least in the sense of a grounding in historical constraints and interests. Obviously, to lose sight of such constraints and interests is, as Stuart Hall has argued, to lose sight of "the relation between culture and questions of hegemony."[1] But to raise questions about power and hegemony is to underline the fundamentally different paths of development that cultural studies have taken in the United States and Britain. Such questions also serve as a reminder that several conflicting and overlapping traditions compete for ascendancy within the broad interpretative sphere of cultural analysis, and that the term *cultural studies* can be attached to any number of projects and programs.

In both the United States and Britain the desire to break free from the tradition-bound and narrowly defined academic disciplines and to set up more inclusive ways of approaching history, culture, and society began to take shape in the late 1940s and 1950s. In practice, however, the ways in which cultural studies developed in each country were very much influenced by the politics of divergent national histories.

The first attempts to institute a form of cultural studies in the United States emerged with the rise of American studies, although this ultimately turned out to be a politically neutral and uncritical mode of interpretation. In Britain the ideal of cultural studies emerged as a critical, interventionist endeavor that formed in opposition to an elitist and exclusionary use of the term *culture*. In practice, this meant that the vast majority of people, along with their experiences, social rituals, habits of thought, modes of expression, and forms of community organization, were systematically excluded from the historical and cultural register and dumped under the sign of the "masses." The task of expanding the concept of culture to include the lives and struggles of working-class groups was thus a political project from the very beginning in the British context, and for the most part, the project was greatly influenced by arguments developed within a Western Marxist tradition. Moreover, there was in Britain a distinct openness toward contemporary popular culture, an area of cultural experience and activity that had been written off by certain sections of both British and American intellectuals as the debased coinage of mass culture. Indeed, within the ideologically charged atmosphere of the Cold War, the American intellectual critique of mass culture took on a decidedly puritanical tone that played well, and was probably designed to play well, with the witch-hunting tendencies of the era.

As Andrew Ross demonstrates in his study of intellectuals and popular culture, the social politics of the Cold War in the United States were shaped in good measure by "intellectuals' contradictory responses to the domestic development of mass-produced popular culture." On the surface, Ross explains, "nothing could seem more perfectly at home in the new prosperity state of post-war consumer capitalism than the domestic forms of the popular culture industries." For many American intellectuals, however, these forms of organized mass culture bore the "foreign" traces of "Stalinized taste" and came to signify an "official distinction between American/UnAmerican, or inside/outside."[2] In many ways, the "containment" of popular culture became a crucial domestic project for many intellectuals, and it was fired with the same kind of ideological urgency as the foreign-policy commitment to militarily contain communism abroad. In such an atmosphere, the concept of culture tended to become more narrowly defined and closed off from considerations of ideology and class.

Similar pressures and burdens were operative in Britain, of course, but the political context, and therefore the intellectual debates, were quite different. For one thing, more vibrant and deeply rooted forms of parliamentary socialism presented institutional as well as political limits to the anti-left hysterics of the American Cold War. Nevertheless, the nascent elements of cultural studies in Britain tended to remain a somewhat marginalized intellectual practice associated with particular individuals, such as Raymond Williams and Richard Hoggart, or with intellectual affiliations that gathered around such Marxist journals as the *New Reasoner* (the "Reasoner" group included E. P. Thompson, Ralph Miliband, and Christopher Hill), and with political movements like the Campaign for Nuclear Disarmament and the New Left, elements of which came together around the *New Left Review* (initially edited by Stuart Hall).[3] It was within such loosely affiliated groups and among individuals, rather than within institutional structures such as the universities, that cultural studies began to take shape in postwar Britain. For many years, only the Center for Contemporary Cultural Studies, founded in 1964 at the University of Birmingham, could be said to offer a relatively stable institutional environment where the intellectual work of cultural studies could be developed.

In the United States during those same years, the American studies ideal produced a markedly different set of methods and procedures. The American studies "movement" was to mushroom into an academic boom in the postwar years and, unlike the embattled and critically disposed forms of British cultural studies, very quickly found institutional and economic support within an expanding university system. One of the consequences of this early success was that American studies never developed any real sense of oppositional cultural criticism and tended to fall into line with the dominant ideological trends of the period.[4] As I argue in this chapter, the consequences of this conformity linked the American studies movement to the wider intellectual and cultural scene as the United States drifted into the Vietnam War.

The initial concern of American studies as it emerged in the 1950s was to synthesize literary studies, history, and the social sciences. The "original goal" of American studies, according to one historian of the movement, was "to study American culture systematically as a whole and yet to do justice to its individual facets."[5] An early expression of this desire was articulated in 1948 by Tremaine McDowell, one of the oft-proclaimed "founding fathers" of the American studies movement: "The discipline of American Studies is the intellectual process whereby a student assimilates the complicated and often contradictory details of American civilization . . . whereby he fashions out of them a picture of these United States. In doing so, he reduces diversity to some degree of unity."[6] McDowell's aim was to establish coherence and order in what only appeared to be diversity and conflict. His procedure, moreover, consisted of forging a synthesis on the level of intellectual inquiry.

Another example of the same "original" view can be found in Richard Huber's 1954 essay "A Theory of American Studies," in which Huber argued that the purpose of the American studies movement was to grasp "reality as a whole" and to analyze "the functional inter-relationships between parts within the whole."[7] The underlying premise was that there existed a fundamental connectedness in American life and that, as a consequence, there was an organic unity to American culture. Thus Huber's position suggested a subtle shift during those early years from attempts to synthesize the surface diversity of American culture to a search for the internal functional links of an organically unified cultural whole. The goal of that exercise, as Roy Harvey Pearce has written, was to form an "integrated, genuinely holistic view" of "American civilization."[8]

Behind these early "holistic" formulations one can easily detect the influence of the dominant political and intellectual currents of the period. In particular, the emphasis on functional interrelationships draws heavily upon the structural-functionalist notion of "core values," that is, a core system of normative values to which the majority adheres, but over which no particular group has control. Under the guidance of Talcott Parsons, Clyde Kluckhohn, and Edward Shils (among others), structural-functionalism held sway in American sociology of the 1950s and 1960s. Furthermore, one can also note the influence of the anthropological concept of superorganicism, in which culture is theorized as an autonomous, extrahuman affair—a concept that had been influential in anthropology since at least the 1920s. Operating in conjunction with these influences, moreover, was the contemporary patriotic desire to articulate the American historical experience and way of life as unique. As Pearce argued the case, "recording, comprehending, and evaluating that uniqueness" defined the central quest of American studies.[9]

As we shall see, during the time of the Vietnam War such ideas, with their unexamined nationalistic underpinnings, would come in for a good deal of criticism and debate. Importantly, American studies also emerged as an oppositional practice to the New Criticism in literary studies. In the shape of "myth symbolism," the dominant mode of literary analysis in the Americanist movement of the 1950s and 1960s, American studies sought to offer a more contextually aware approach to the analysis of literary texts. Whereas the extreme formalism of New Criticism tended to reify literature, divorcing it from any consideration of sociopolitical influences, myth symbolism was determined to historicize literature. Broadly speaking, myth symbolism conceptualized myths as expressions of the dominant forms of thought of a given era; they were the "collective representations" or symbolic expressions that embodied the ideals and aspirations of the American people as a whole in particular historical periods.[10] But in this move toward history and contextual analysis, American studies also confronted its own fears of becoming simply an adjunct to sociology or anthropology, and hence it retreated to established disciplinary boundaries.

Henry Nash Smith articulated this fear in his 1957 essay on the problems of developing a theory of American studies. Sociology, he contended, was incapable of dealing with the uniqueness of literature, and anthropology was unable to "take account of the full range of meanings available to us in the arts of complex modern societies such as our own." Seeing no way forward with the two established approaches to society and culture, Nash fell back on the claims of the humanist literary critic: "Is it not conceivable that the masterpiece of literature, or the exceptionally productive career" are the most valid expressions of culture, which can move beyond the content analysis of sociology and beyond the scope of "merely average life-patterns" to reach the root meaning of a particular historical moment?[11] Within the institutional version of American studies, however, moving beyond the "merely average" and into the "valid expressions of culture" entailed a selective process of canon formation that borrowed, for the most part, from F. O. Matthiessen's influential yet narrowly defined notion of American "Renaissance" literature. The resulting list of "great works," while suggesting a seamless evolution of American letters, did not go very far toward illuminating the cultural conflicts that littered the politics of literature in the nineteenth century.[12]

Thus from Smith's essay we can deduce a method (close textual reading) and an object of study ("the masterpieces of literature") that demonstrate just how much early Americanists were in thrall to the Cold War forms of literary studies. In this view, *culture* remained a vague and untheorized term that merely provided a convenient background to frame exceptionally productive careers. Pragmatic and piecemeal ways of studying literature in culture (the latter now stripped of any consideration of ideological effects), rather than a concern for the cultural process itself, appear to have been the order of the day. American culture simply existed, or at least could be somehow located, in what was variously referred to as the "American experience" or the "American mind." And the fundamental indices to the "main currents" of American culture were assumed to exist in the canonized masterpieces of the "American Renaissance."

History, too, was kept at a distance, as Myra Jehlen has noted, and tended to be treated as selective context or background noise "rather than as an integral part of the literary language." In this way, history devolved "into either disparate facts or all-encompassing trends that tend to confirm the established readings." Thus, the myth symbolists tended to elide both the ideological dimension of literature as well as its representations of social contradictions.[13] Jehlen views this elision of the actualities of the historical record as a function of the general ideological conformity of the 1950s. Certainly, the dominant trend in the study of American history itself during those years was "neoconservative," linked to the "consensus school" of historical explanation—an approach to the American past that celebrated an assumed continuity of liberal-Lockean values about which there had always existed an overwhelming consensus. The desire to represent the dynamics of the American experience in terms of continuity and consensus—as a uniquely "contradiction-free" branch of human evolution—was therefore not exclusive to American studies. It was, rather, the dominant intellectual, political, and thus ideological paradigm of the Cold War. In the making at the same time, however, was a series of subcultural or countercultural movements that would shatter this paradigm during the following decade: notably, the civil rights movement, feminism, and the emerging youth movement. The Vietnam War would force these potentially volatile social compounds together for a brief explosive moment in the late 1960s, before splitting them apart again in the changed conditions of the 1970s and 1980s.

In terms of cultural theory, several developments within the social sciences generally, and within segments of the American studies movement specifically, began to take shape in the late 1950s. One of the most influential books to appear shortly before that time was the encyclopedic survey *Culture: A Critical Review of Concepts and Methods* (1952), written jointly by A. L. Kroeber (the originator of the term *superorganic*) and Clyde Kluckhohn.Central to that widely read and often quoted study was the belief that the epistemological underpinnings of the social sciences ought to be based on the concept of culture.[14] Clearly, within American studies a general interest in cultural theory began to emerge as Kroeber and Kluckhohn's survey was being absorbed into the academy. In 1958 Robert Walker's *American Studies in the United States* appeared as the first book-length study to propose cultural anthropology as an area most likely to supply American studies with a method capable of comprehending American culture as a whole. In Walker's view, borrowing from cultural anthropology would make it possible for American studies to construct a "single comprehensive method for examining and organizing the multi-fold data and phenomena which describes a group of people living in a given place at a given time."[15] That holistic approach to American culture, proposed by Walker via Kroeber's superorganic theory of culture, suggested a direction for American studies that was less oriented toward literary texts and the liberal humanism of the myth symbolists.

In 1963 Richard E. Sykes developed Walker's suggestions in his essay "American Studies and the Concept of Culture: A Theory and Method." In that essay, superorganicism was a major influence, as was Kroeber and Kluckhohn's definition of culture as an "abstract description of trends toward uniformity in words, acts, and artifacts of human groups."[16] Having established a definition of culture, Sykes proceeded to answer the question, What then is American Studies? as follows: "Briefly defined, it is the study of American culture. Culture is the key concept, the unifying concept, the root word which suggests both theory and method. It is a branch of cultural studies, and as such is closer to the social sciences than to the humanities. It is a specialized branch of cultural anthropology."[17] Although by no means completely jettisoning humanistic criticism or imaginative literature as the central object of study, Sykes nevertheless insisted that the American studies approach to literature should be "that of the student of culture, not the critic."[18] In spite of his borrowings from cultural anthropology, there was little indication that American studies was about to shift much closer than it already had to the social sciences or that it would develop a more critically disposed form of cultural study. Indeed, the interest in culture theory can be seen in many ways as an attempt to bolster traditional literary concerns with the trappings of scientific theory. That becomes clearer when we examine the theory in question and note the historical changes at work within it.

As we have seen, both Walker and Sykes borrowed Kroeber's concept of superorganicism, but their contact with that theory was through the jointly written survey *Culture: A Critical Review of Concepts and Methods,* in which Kluckhohn's more idealist views were paramount.[19] This is not to say that Kroeber was a materialist. As with most students of Franz Boas (one of the founders of anthropology in the United States), materialist strategies were either ignored or opposed. However, Kroeber's initial definition of culture, written in 1917, was not far removed from Edward Tylor's original nineteenth-century formulation of a "complex whole" that included technological and environmental determinants as well as ideas and values. But by the time Kroeber came to co-author *Culture* in 1952, his definition of culture, although it retained notions of "patterns of behavior," had become more narrowly idealist: "the essential core of culture consists of traditional . . . ideas and especially their attached values."[20] When Walker came to publish *American Studies* in 1958, Kroeber's culture concept had undergone yet another change, this time under the influence of Talcott Parsons. As one of the chief spokespersons for structural functionalism in the 1950s, Parsons laid great emphasis on the ways societies maintain themselves through the imposition of rules, values, norms, and specific goals. Parsons's position of importance as cofounder with Kluckhohn of Harvard University's Department of Social Relations guaranteed that his structural functionalism would be influential in the social sciences in general and on Kroeber's work in particular. Thus, when Parsons and Kroeber came to co-author the essay "The Concept of Culture and of Social Systems" in 1958, Kroeber's initial concept of "complex whole" and "patterns of behavior" had been reduced to "patterns of values, ideas and other symbolic-meaningful systems."[21] Therefore, by the time that Walker and Sykes came to Kroeber's work, it had already become saturated by a narrow idealism, stemming mostly from the structural functionalism of Parsons and Kluckhohn.

As I have noted, these shifts in cultural theory and changes in social analysis reflect historical changes in the nature of American domestic politics and America's status as a post–World War II global power—a status defined by the terms of a strident anticommunism. By the 1950s a wholesale revision of previous social theory was changing the basic premises of intellectual inquiry. Topics that had been quite common before the war, such as the nature and function of political power or the class nature of economic relations, had been all but eradicated from the social sciences by the 1960s. In their place was a theory of pluralism, which conceptualized American society as a complex network of interest groups that competed in the political arena on a more or less equal footing. Regardless of whether the interest group was a particular industry or a group of citizens who shared certain needs, all were assumed to have equal access to and influence over the political process through the ballot and through lobbying. The fundamental reason for the continuity of pluralism, it was claimed, was the existence of a broadly based normative consensus on core values. It was then further argued that ideology—that problematic import from Europe—no longer functioned in American society. Ideology, in other words, had been transcended thanks to the pluralism of American society.[22] As a tool for explaining American history, society, and culture, as well as personality structure and behavioral patterns, notions of pluralism dominated the academy from the late 1940s to the late 1960s.[23]

Commenting critically on the theory of pluralism from the perspective of British cultural studies, Stuart Hall has written that although the approach was "advanced as empirically grounded and scientific," it was nevertheless "predicated on a very specific set of political and ideological presuppositions." Hall explained: "These presuppositions, however, were not put to the test, within the theory, but framed and underpinned it as a set of unexamined postulates. It should have asked, 'Does pluralism work?' and 'how does pluralism work?' Instead, it asserted 'pluralism works'—and then went on to measure, precisely and empirically, just how well it was doing." Hall's main complaint was that the pluralist denial of structural or class barriers in the United States rested on "a mixture of prophecy and hope" dressed up as "pure science." The result of these dubious assumptions was that the pluralists missed altogether the multitude of unabsorbed elements "still simmering in the American melting pot."[24]

The general theoretical changes that so mark the social sciences of the 1950s and 1960s were as much political and ideological as intellectual in nature, and go some way toward explaining the changes in Kroeber's work. What American studies was borrowing from was not a value-free practice of history, sociology or anthropology, but a new and historically specific form of those practices—a neoconservative historiography and a liberal pluralist social science. As Leo Marx commented in 1979, American studies was born in the 1930s of a "New Deal anti-fascist version of progressivism" when the assumption was that "the crisis of capitalism brought on by the Great Depression and the menace of fascism would be resolved by making democracy an economic as well as a juridical and legislative reality." But, Marx explained, the "1930s sense of social purpose and idealism" was lost sight of in the postwar years for a number of reasons: the emergence of American studies in the academy took place on "the wave of overheated nationalism" that accompanied the Cold War; the effects of the "imperial power" that America enjoyed after World War II, and the subsequent role of "scholarly ambassadors" conferred upon practitioners of American studies by the Fulbright Act and the State Department; and the subsequent rise of a "politically antiseptic, disengaged scholarly mode" that came to characterize American studies as a discipline.[25]

The 1950s form of American studies, however, with its roots in literary criticism and underpinnings of pluralism, was shattered by the upheavals of the Vietnam War era. Indeed, as I have already suggested, the assumptions of the post–World War II period in general, and the pluralist theories of society in particular, were not "destined to survive the testing times of the ghetto rebellions, campus revolts, counter-culture upheavals, and anti-war movements of the late 1960s."[26] In the changed conditions of this confrontational era, the internal American studies debates over culture and history grew increasingly intense as entrenched methods and procedures came under sustained attack. Whereas the older generation of Americanists had seen themselves as creating havens for "free, inquiring minds," the younger generation was more likely to view the whole project as an "overly timid and elitist white Protestant male enterprise which tended to reinforce the dominant culture rather than critically analyze it."[27] The legitimizing myths of pastoral innocence in which American cultural values were said to have developed seemed grossly inadequate in the face of the Vietnam War, political assassinations, and urban riots.[28] How could concepts such as the "American Adam" be balanced against the slaughter of Vietnamese villagers at My Lai, the assassinations of Martin Luther King, Jr., and Robert Kennedy, and the shooting of the students at Kent State and Jackson State? And how could the notion of American exceptionalism, that central ideological trope in early American studies writing, maintain its intellectual allure when the most glaring facts of the age portrayed the United States as an interventionist military power motivated by global economic imperatives?

The American studies celebration of America's "Adamic" origins could not be squared with demands for sexual, racial, and class equality in the late 1960s and early 1970s. Such sexualized metaphors as the "virgin land," for example, which represented the Western frontier in terms of male conquest over a passive female continent, were simply no longer tolerable.[29] The Western frontier was now more likely to be thought of as a "fatal environment" that, in Richard Slotkin's terms, invoked the Vietnam War as "our last great Indian war" and revealed at the same time the "Frontier Myth's dark side of racism, false pride, and the profligate wastage of lives, cultures, and resources."[30]

Of course, these insights, revisions, and developments were not the exclusive concern of American studies. A general atmosphere of suspicion, unrest, and confrontation characterized the academy of the 1960s and early 1970s. As the war in Vietnam dragged on, in spite of an ever-escalating domestic opposition, the institutions of higher learning became the focus of a widespread discontent. For many students and educators the universities were exposed "as both locked into and paradigmatic of wider structures of dehumanizing bureaucracy, complicit with military violence and technological exploitation."[31] Surveying those years in relation to American studies, Gene Wise notes:

After the middle of the sixties, it was hard to assume without question that America is an integrated whole; division and conflict, not consensus, seemed to characterize the culture. It was also difficult to assume the privileged position of elite ideas as a window into culture. Hard facts—emotionally searing events like assassinations and riots, gigantic institutions which could wreak havoc on people's lives—these held power, it appeared, to create or destroy an insubstantial idea in a flash. Students of America thus turned away from airy myths and symbols to look at earthier matters . . . at functioning social structures like the family or the city or the town or school or corporation or labor union or prison, at measurable human behavior and at people's life-styles.[32]

Wise concluded that American studies never fully recovered from "the earthquake-like jolts of the sixties and the consciousness those events forced upon the culture."[33] As with other academic disciplines, American studies blossomed with radical caucuses, alternative practices, and oppositional journals.[34]

And yet instead of producing a comprehensive alternative to the liberal humanist and pluralist assumptions of the older generation of Americanists, American studies experienced a further splintering of the movement. At the same time, other disciplines within the humanities, especially history and literary studies, began to broaden their theoretical horizons in the wake of the events of the 1960s. The influence of British social history and cultural studies, and of continental theory from structuralism to postmodernism, meant that the dominant "texts in context" approach of American studies no longer offered a compelling or very far-reaching approach to cultural studies. Looking back at this moment in the history of American studies, Leo Marx noted with a measure of sadness that "with the benefit of hindsight, we can see that a truly imaginative American Studies enterprise just possibly might have obviated the demand for separate Afro-American Studies and Women's Studies in the 1960s."[35]

In the aftermath of the 1960s, then, a range of new perspectives and problems resulted in a new cycle of borrowing and synthesizing that would eventually lead some Americanists toward more critical forms of cultural studies, including the British culturalist approach. For the most part, however, American studies as a movement and pedagogical practice tended to steer clear of radical foreign imports.

OUT OF THE SIXTIES

An example of the new kinds of syntheses taking place in American studies in the post-Vietnam era came in 1974 with the publication of R. Gordon Kelly's essay "Literature and the Historian." Setting out to construct a more fully developed, social-scientific approach to American culture and to cultural evidence, Kelly insisted that if we were to understand the historical processes that govern the production and consumption of texts, then we needed "more inclusive concepts of culture, and more complex social models than are implicit in the doctrine of literary power."[36] The theoretical approach that Kelly proposed was a compilation drawn from the anthropological theories of Clifford Geertz and Anthony F. C. Wallace, and the phenomenological social theory of Peter Berger and Thomas Luckmann. From Geertz he borrowed the notion of "cultural knowledge," which consists of culturally specific "control mechanisms—plans, recipes, rules, instructions—for the governing of behavior."[37] It is through these control mechanisms that individuals and groups relate to one another and to their environment. Through a close study of "cultural knowledge" or the controlling system of symbols, Kelly claimed, we arrive at what has significance and value for a particular group in culture. However, those "structures of meaning" differ greatly between groups within a given social formation. Thus no individual or group has access to the full range of knowledge in a particular culture.

For this reason Kelly introduced Wallace's cognitive anthropology, in which sociocultural systems were theorized as the "organization of diversity." In this scheme, culture operates "with a minimal level of cognitive sharing."[38] Kelly argued that given the complexity of American culture and the subsequent diversity of cultural knowledge, it would seem "unwarranted to conceive of American society as a unitary culture for the purpose of historical analysis or to define a handful of literary figures as qualitatively superior cultural informants."[39] Hence, he claimed, we need to take into account the historical and cultural factors that shape the production and consumption of literary texts.

Kelly cautioned that we also bear in mind that the text will have a different range of meanings depending on the perceptual and conceptual competence of diverse cultural knowledge groups. But how, one might ask, is meaning produced in culture? Kelly responded that meaning is "a function of the author's belief system and of the group to which he belongs." Historical meaning in literature, the traditional object of study for the myth symbolists, consists of a mixture of authorial intent and what we would now perhaps term reader-response criticism, "circumscribed within specific, and hence necessarily limited, conceptual frameworks."[40] In other words, historical meaning is mediated unevenly within culture, and therefore literary meaning does not operate uniformly across diverse configurations of intercultural cognitive structures. However, given Kelly's previous adherence to Geertz's theory of symbolically mediated social reality and to Wallace's theory of "minimal cognitive sharing," how is one to formulate a concept of "real" historical-cultural contexts? Kelly found the answer in Berger and Luckmann's *The Social Construction of Reality* (1967).

As the title of that book suggests, reality for Berger and Luckmann is not an ontological category; rather, reality is theorized in terms of structured systems of meaning that are collectively produced within the social formation and culturally maintained. Moreover, "reality" as a socially constructed symbolic system is held together by the most important of all symbolic systems—language. Given the precariousness of those arbitrary symbolic structures, however, the individual's relationship to the environment is in all times and places "imperfectly structured" by the human biological constitution, and related only tendentiously to material and to technological and environmental factors.[41] The validity and continuity of this systemic social reality can be maintained only through the strict acculturation of the young, who must be taught to relate to the world as it is constructed by the group.[42]

Although Kelly did not displace literature from its privileged status as the primary object of study in American studies, he did go some way toward rethinking the process of literary production and consumption as a cultural practice. Taking a closer look at the theoretical foundations of Kelly's argument, however, a number of shortcomings appear, which stem from his borrowed concepts and theories.

By employing Berger and Luckmann's phenomenological model of reality, for example, Kelly posited a social theory that held that there are only minimal interrelationships between social forms and reality. Thus he ignored any notion of infrastructural or technological and environmental influences, and he refused to engage the question of institutional influences on social forms and the subsequent issues of power and hegemony. Only consciousness as it creates symbolic realities was of interest to Berger and Luckmann, with the result that they tended to reduce everything to subjective processes within an ahistorical model of language. Accordingly, they found no meaning in reality except that which social groups subjectively create for themselves in order to maintain the status quo.

Such an approach to cultural structures of perception also failed to account for the historical roots of, or specific motivations for, symbolic social maintenance systems, any more than it explained why certain meanings become dominant at certain times or in whose interest such meanings serve. That failure left Kelly's project with an interpretative theory of meaning but no explanation of how meaning is produced, reproduced, and distributed, or how it operates to mediate change or reconcile conflict within the Geertz-Wallace model of minimally sharing cognitive structures, groups, and individuals. Finally, it missed entirely the fragmenting processes of culture and ideology, which creates fractures and conflicts along the experiential lines of gender, race, and class.

Geertz, on the other hand, viewed culture as a system of understandable symbols—a context in which acts are signs that can be interpreted semiotically. He rejected holistic and material concepts of culture in favor of a more narrowly conceived performative notion of social discourse. What interested Geertz was cultural behavior viewed as a discursive and symbolically structured phenomenon that can be decoded linguistically. Thus the guiding premise of Geertz's theory was that of "culture as text," but the focus of his procedure was on what was already written. Geertz seemed little interested in the material or social production of writing, in the historical processes of discourse, or in the limiting conventions and political expediences of rhetoric and representation. Instead, he understood culture as an accomplished text, as an already achieved symbolic practice endlessly spinning webs of signification across the surface of observable social interaction.[43] His procedure failed to explain the deeper cultural or wider historical forces at work within a social formation, whether thickly described or not.

None of Kelly's sources, therefore, appeared much interested in the cultural forms or social practices of power, dominance, legitimation, selection, or control (except in the abstract, depoliticized sense of symbolic rules or recipes). None tackled the problem of change, contradiction, oppositional activity, and conflict. Moreover, by narrowing his concept of culture in order to repudiate the holistic approach of the myth symbolists, Kelly was in danger of slipping into a form of existentialism. For although we can agree that the myth-symbolist notion of a unitary culture constituted consensually around core values is no longer a particularly viable one, that need not then compel us to assume, with the cognitive theorists, that culture consists of a multitude of diverse realities that share little or nothing in common. In culture, as in society, everything is at some level connected to everything else, even though this may not always appear to be the case. The rediscovery of conflicts and contradictions, outgroups and subcultures in the 1960s certainly undermined the pluralist, neoconservative, and structural-functionalist concept of culture, but it would be a mistake to assume thereafter that those conflicts and outgroups were somehow outside of culture, when the point is that they are crucial structuring elements of culture.

Finally, by setting up a theory of culture that privileged language, Kelly's theoretical synthesis highlighted a fundamental process of all cultures: the production of meaningful systems of communication and signification. But this proposition needed to be taken a step further. For to claim that cultures were marked by an uneven distribution of "cultural knowledge," based on the relationship of groups and individuals to the controlling system of symbols, was also to propose a hierarchical social system based on a relationship to the production of meaning. In other words, meaning in culture was not an innocent or value-free affair, as Berger and Luckmann would probably agree, but was a specific product of historically constituted social relationships. And because meaning was the product of social relationships and practices, and was not a naturally occurring phenomenon, it was also ideological. Berger and Luckmann, and Geertz for that matter, tended to reduce ideology to secondary systems of ideas—a notion that, not surprisingly, was close to the myth-symbolist understanding.[44] However, precisely because meaning is never innocent—because it is always a product of particular ways of constructing reality—ideology must be understood as something more than mere "ideas." A more useful approach is one that views ideologies in terms of actual social practices that constitute material forces in everyday life, producing concrete effects in both subjectivity and signification.

To introduce concepts of this nature is to move beyond the theoretical scope of Kelly's essay into what Stuart Hall has termed "the critical paradigm" of cultural studies—a paradigm that emerged with the "rediscovery" of the ideological dimension of culture.[45] The emergence of a critical cultural studies in Britain involved various theoretical and disciplinary approaches, including linguistics, semiotics, structuralism, and psychoanalysis. Stuart Hall's work registered this synthesis most strikingly, bringing together as it did the historical approach of E. P. Thompson, the theories of ideology developed by Antonio Gramsci and Louis Althusser, and the post-Gramscian, post-Althusserian concept of hegemony associated with the writings of Raymond Williams—specifically, with Williams's notion of dominant, residual, and emergent cultural elements.[46]

It is therefore fitting that a discussion of British cultural studies begin with the writings of Stuart Hall and Raymond Williams. Indeed, although their work has become central to contemporary debates about the politics of culture ("cultural materialism" in Williams's terms), both Hall and Williams emerged from the margins of "official" English culture. As a black Caribbean in a predominantly white intellectual world, Hall has managed to maintain a distance from the less critical theoretical trends that swept across Europe and Britain in the disillusioning aftermath of the late 1960s. Like Williams, who came from a Welsh working-class background, Hall has consistently attended to the effective power of politics and culture (and the politics of culture), and to the very real material struggles and structures of resistance that permeate the actualities of everyday life. Thus, for all of their grasp of complex theoretical systems of thought, Williams's and Hall's experiences, sympathies, and affiliations have always worked against the blinding embrace of "theory for theory's sake."[47]

A CRITICAL PARADIGM FOR CULTURAL STUDIES

What I am proposing as a "critical paradigm" for cultural studies begins, by way of an analysis of the work of Williams and Hall, with the concept of culture itself. Unlike many of the theorists surveyed thus far, however, those British culturalists did not approach culture as though its meanings were straightforward or stable or somehow removed from the problematics of the theories in which they are constituted. Raymond Williams addressed just that issue when he wrote:

At the very centre of a major area of modern thought and practice . . . is a concept, "culture," which in itself, through variation and complication, embodies not only the issues but the contradictions through which it has developed. The concept at once fuses and confuses the radically different experiences and tendencies of its formation. It is then impossible to carry through any serious analysis without reaching towards a consciousness of the concept itself: a consciousness that must be . . . historical.[48]

The problem, therefore, was that the culture concept appeared as a richly developed theory, as a fully achieved practice, when in fact what actually existed was an ongoing debate over the meaning of culture as a structuring process and its relationship to the social formation. Seen from this perspective, the most basic concepts were best understood not as concepts at all but as problems. Furthermore, as Williams explained, those were "not analytic problems either but historical movements which are still unresolved."[49] The first task of thinking critically about culture thus involved working through the historically changing nature of the concept itself in order to recover the "substance" from the forms of its different usages. For the term *culture* has served several historically specific functions, as Williams noted:

> Beginning as a noun of process—the culture (cultivation) of crops or (rearing and breeding) of animals, and by extension the culture (active cultivation) of the human mind—it became in the late eighteenth century, especially in German and English, a noun of "configuration" or "generalization," of the "spirit" which informed the "whole way of life" of a distinct people.[50]

This latter sense of the term informed the roots of anthropology and was associated with Edward Tylor's pioneering nineteenth-century holistic formulation. Another way of expressing the term (cultivation of the mind) was to convey a sense of those things in life other than the then-industrializing political economy. In this sense, too, it stood for the aristocratic and high-bourgeois opposition to the expanding enfranchisement of the "masses." This kind of usage, usually associated with Matthew Arnold, upheld "Culture" ("the best knowledge and thought of the time") as an alternative aesthetic sphere of taste and high art that stood apart from the crass materialism of the bourgeois industrial order, and also as an elite realm of educational refinement that was beyond the reach of the industrialized working masses.[51] In changed and continually changing forms, both of these usages continue to exercise influence in the modern world: culture as a way of life, and culture as a standard of excellence.

Whereas the kinds of culture theory that American studies tended to borrow from (Geertz, Wallace, and Berger) tended to narrow down the culture concept, Williams was convinced that Tylor's formula of a "complex whole" was nearer to the actual lived conditions of a culture. When studying real relationships in actual analysis, Williams insisted, there always comes a point when we realize that what is being studied is "a general organization in a particular example, and that in this general organization there is no element that we can abstract and separate from the rest." What Williams called the study of culture, then, was the study of relationships in a whole way of life. No single element could be abstracted without distorting the relational existence of all the other elements. Therefore, because art, for example, was produced within society, there could be "no solid whole" outside of society "to which we concede priority." It was an error, wrote Williams, "to suppose that values or art-works" could be "adequately studied without reference to the particular society within which they were (are) expressed"; they existed in society "as an activity, with the production, the trading, the politics, the raising of families."[52]

The "critical paradigm" thus began from the premise that culture cannot be studied in terms of autonomous artifacts or practices. Instead, culture was theorized as a process through which meaning is produced, dispersed, and historically transformed; it therefore affects all activities at every level of the social formation. Consequently, culture was viewed not as a static phenomenon or an a priori category, but rather as "a field of mutually if also unevenly determining forces."[53] The by-now-classic conceptual tool for understanding this process, and one that underlined its political dimension, was the concept of *hegemony.* Importantly, the concept of hegemony did not reduce cultural studies to a form of political science, as Giles Gunn has noted, but it did "compel students of culture to raise new questions about what might be called [culture's] politics of organization."[54]

The idea of hegemony, as it was articulated theoretically in British cultural studies, was first proposed by Antonio Gramsci as a way of explaining the noncoercive ways in which ruling-class groups maintain their dominance over, and even win the allegiance of, the "subaltern" classes.[55] The work of hegemony attempts to impose ideological domination over the sociocultural formation, and to organize mass consent systematically according to the prevailing status quo. That attempt requires constant adjustments and shifts in tactics and strategies in order to win, and rewin, a people's acceptance of a system that does not, in practice, necessarily ensure that their needs and interests will be accommodated. *Hegemony,* then, refers at once to historically specific coalitions of dominant groups and also to the persistent work necessary to persuade and orchestrate the will of the majority in line with the needs of established power blocs.

The concept of hegemony in British culturalism represented a qualified break with the classic Marxist base-superstructure model and the economic determinism that came to be associated with Marxism during the period of the Second International. In that model, sociocultural activity had been seen as merely a by-product, a reflection or ideological expression of the economically determining base. The break with that model did not represent a rejection of determinism altogether, however, but rather shifted the emphasis from a prefigured economic determinism to the sociocultural processes of selection, persuasion, and incorporation—the exertion of pressures and the setting of limits. In other words, the concept of hegemony suggested the dialectic between "social being" and "social consciousness" without collapsing one term into the other. In this way, base and superstructure were reconstituted not as separate entities but as dialectically interwined processes. That dialectic, as Williams pointed out, is effective in all "social and economic relationships" and contains "fundamental contradictions and variations"; it is, therefore, "always in a state of dynamic process."[56] As the upheavals of the 1960s demonstrated, that dynamic process produces oppositional political practice and new forms of social identity.

Culture, then, came to be seen as this dialectic; it is a dynamically active process and, as such, is intimately involved in the ideological nature of the social production of meaning. Again, the point was that ideology cannot be separated from culture; it is not, as Catherine Belsey explained, "an optional extra, deliberately adopted by selfconscious individuals," but is instead "the very condition of our experience of the world."[57] Following from the work of Louis Althusser, British culturalists challenged "positivist" and "historicist" theories originally formulated by Karl Marx in *The German Ideology*. For Marx, ideology represented a separate phenomenon from the material conditions of everyday life, in much the same way that dreams were once thought, prior to Freud, to represent "pure illusion" or arbitrary remnants left over from the actualities of lived experience. Thus ideology for Marx was "an imaginary assemblage (*bricolage*), a pure dream, empty and vain, constituted by the day's residues from the only full and positive reality, that of the concrete history of concrete material individuals materially producing their existence."[58] Althusser, on the other hand, whose work exerted a profound influence on British culturalism, argued that ideologies form a complex system of images, representations, myths, concepts, and ideas that provide cultures with their structures of perception, through which the experience of reality is organized. In Althusser's view, ideology is quite literally our way of thinking, conceptualizing, speaking, and experiencing; it is the "omnipresent and transhistorical" structures of social knowledge; it is the world of signs and practices that bind individuals to the social structure and, moreover, center them as subjects within a lived sense of purpose and identity.[59]

Importantly, according to Althusser, language represents

the fundamental process through which that "centering" is achieved. For it is only through the learned ability to manipulate the signs and signifying practices of language that individuals make sense of their experiences. To be sure, language is always populated with the intentions of others—which is a way of saying that language is an already functioning process of intentions and meanings as far as the individual subject of culture is concerned.[60] Edward Said had something like this in mind when he wrote that the very possibility of culture is premised on the notion of power, and power is maintained by virtue of domination over the selective processes of culture:

> Arnold's thesis that culture is the best that is thought or said gives this notion its most compact form. Culture is an instrument for identifying, selecting, and affirming certain "good" things, forms, practices, or ideas over others and in so doing culture transmits, diffuses, partitions, teaches, presents, propagates, persuades and above all it creates and recreates itself as specialized apparatus for doing all these things.[61]

Here Said confirms the proposition found in the work of Williams and Hall that culture is an "institutionalized process" in which what is considered appropriate to it is kept appropriate, and that which is considered inappropriate is silenced, marginalized, and positioned as "other." The seemingly natural process of selection, its procedures for the most part obscured, is nevertheless the result of actual social practices, activities, and relationships. The power in and of culture stems from the ability to legitimate, validate, differentiate and, most importantly, to designate the boundaries by which what is acceptable is conceptualized in relation to its projected opposite. It is in this sense that we can say that culture contains dominant modes of discourse, which are sustained through prevailing codes, systems, and structures. But to recognize that dominant discourses exist in culture is also to recognize the existence of subordinate discursive realms—those that the dominant modes must actively undermine in a continual demonstration of superior virtues and values.

The recognition of culture as a "contested terrain" (the "dialectic of cultural struggle," as Stuart Hall described it) has become a central focus in critical cultural studies in recent years.[62] Extending that view, I would argue that during periods of cultural crisis, such as the Gilded Age, the Great Depression, or the Vietnam War era, dominant cultural forms become increasingly difficult to maintain and alternative forms are less easily dismissed. In such periods of crisis, the hegemonic process of securing popular consent is disrupted, and the negotiations between dominant and subordinate values break down. In this sense, as Gramsci explained, a crisis of the ruling hegemonic system occurs either because the dominant class formation "has failed in some major political undertaking for which it has requested or forcibly extracted the consent of the broad masses" or because large sections of the masses have "passed suddenly from a state of political passivity to a certain activity, and put forward demands which, taken together, albeit not organically formulated, add up to a revolution."[63]

Obviously, the crisis of the Vietnam War and the upheavals of the 1960s did not generate a revolution in the sense of a violent overturning of the prevailing norms of the dominant cultural groups and discourses. But they did create what Gramsci termed a "general crisis of the state" from which the American system has yet to fully recover. Moreover, the oppositional practices of the 1960s, which extended across the social spectrum, and the subsequent political reactions, which eventually lead to the Watergate scandal, did create a "crisis of authority" as many Americans moved from a state of ideological passivity to a politics of active criticism. As the authors of *Policing the Crisis* explain in their study of post–World War II Britain,

A crisis of hegemony marks a moment of profound rupture in the political and economic life of a society, an accumulation of contradictions. If, in moments of hegemony everything works spontaneously so as to sustain and enforce a particular form of class domination while rendering the basis of that social authority invisible through the mechanisms of the production of consent, the moments when the equilibrium of consent is disturbed ... are moments when the whole basis of political leadership and cultural authority become exposed and contested.[64]

The powerful cultural processes, then, that continually strive to orchestrate the hegemonic horizon of credibility and domination do not form an entirely infallible, all-encompassing edifice—and here is an important qualification to Althusserian theories of ideology. For as Raymond Williams argued, historical periods are structured by the mediations and dynamic tensions between dominant, residual, and emergent cultural elements. Primary among these, as I have already suggested, are the dominant or hegemonic structures, which continually attempt to set and define the limits to meaning and value. But at the same time, there are residual elements of the past, derived from former social constructions that are still active and variable in the present. In most cases, residual values are absorbed into the dominant, or have been constructed in such ways as to make them "quaint" and of no threat to the hegemonic order.

Emergent elements are those new meanings, values, practices, relationships, and kinds of relationships. Very often these will constitute new phases of the dominant order as it adjusts to new modes of production and exchange. Sometimes these elements are oppositional and resist incorporation into the dominant order. These elements are what Williams called "the emergent-unincorporated." Segments of the 1960s radicalism, the civil rights, feminist, and antiwar movements can be seen as emergent in this oppositional sense. However, as Williams pointed out, although "new meanings and values ... are continually being created ... there is (now) a much earlier attempt to incorporate them, just because they are part—and yet not a defined part—of effective contemporary practice." Indeed, one of the significant changes in contemporary life is "how very early this attempt is, how alert the dominant culture now is to anything that can be seen as emergent."[65] Hall made a similar point when he warned that no cultural form is forever fixed in its original meaning and practice: "This year's radical symbol or slogan will be neutralized into next year's fashion; the year after, it will be the object of a profound cultural nostalgia."[66] Although Hall was not here addressing the specific manipulations and appropriations of the oppositional sensibilities of the 1960s, his analysis, like Williams's, was obviously applicable to the selective rearticulations of that era across a wide range of cultural forms.

The process of selective incorporation by the dominant cultural order helps to explain the ways in which certain of the emergent sensibilities of the 1960s and the Vietnam War experience have been picked up by the various "gatekeeping" institutions of the dominant culture and the culture industries. A figure like Rambo, for example, would appear to be utterly complicit with the conservative reaction to precautionary American diplomacy in the aftermath of Vietnam. At the same time, however, Rambo evokes the unstable identity of the Vietnam veteran—an identity that haunted the media culture of the 1970s—while his costume (long hair, headband, backpack, etc.) also suggests something of the sixties counterculture and its critique of American society. Moreover, Rambo consistently elicits audience sympathy, positioned as he is in opposition to such official structures of power as local law and order, the military hierarchy, politicians, and the CIA.[67] Thus even a seemingly ideologically transparent figure such as Rambo can invoke a number of correspondences to residual alternative or emergent unincorporated meanings—and this regardless of how carefully such images or themes are initially framed or positioned.

To put the argument yet another way: Dominant cultural modes, as evidenced by the emergent practices of the late 1960s, are not able to contain or exhaust all oppositional or emergent efforts. By the end of the sixties, the breakdown of the "establishment's" ability to control the array of emergent energies and intentions was demonstrated across the proverbial cultural board. It emerged in the area of civil rights, in ethnic power movements, in feminism, in gay activism, and in militant labor unionism. It expressed itself in film, fashion, music, and sexuality. And it emerged in the form of collective political and cultural activism such as mass rallies and moratoriums, boycotts, community politics, sit-ins, teach-ins, and various experiments with alternative forms of communal life-styles. Overall, there opened up a seemingly impassable divide between cultural generations, and there emerged an abiding mistrust of traditional forms of leadership and authority. In addition, there also developed a pointed critique of the "good things" that the dominant culture had selected and paraded as signs of its virtuous superiority.

A great deal of the subsequent expenditure of energy by sections of the dominant groups in the American sociocultural formation has been, and continues to be, devoted to eliminating or incorporating the efforts of that period. (Indeed, it is in this context that a figure like Rambo must be viewed.) The focus of this effort is often generalized as the "Vietnam syndrome," which, as I have suggested, is a term that conjures up for the conservatives of the New Right all that American society is in need of a cure from, as it also connotes the alternative desires and emergent intentions that were generated by the experiences of the Vietnam War era and that remain variously active in the present. The struggle between those two meanings is most centrally ideological, and it constitutes a major structuring problematic in post-Vietnam America. Moreover, not only is it a conflict over signs and meanings, but it is also most crucially a struggle over the cultural power to decide upon the meaning of America—and America's past—in the modern world.

It is on this basis that I have questioned early approaches to American studies and drawn upon British culturalism in an effort to suggest a more critical approach to the study of culture. For if there is a single historical fact, it is that every sociocultural order is governed by the power and authority of hegemonic groups. And if there has been a single significant silence in American studies, it has been on the question of power and the legitimizing cultural processes that make the exercise of power possible. Leo Marx spoke directly to this issue in an essay that addressed the "enervations" of

American studies following the crisis of the Vietnam era. If the history of American studies has a moral, Marx wrote in 1979, then that moral "should have something to do with the relations between intellectuals and power." That moral should remind us, he continued, "of the debilitating effect these relations can have upon the life of the mind when their existence is unexamined or denied."[68] British cultural theorists, such as Williams and Hall, clearly recognized the need for intellectual and critical self-consciousness long before practitioners of American studies in the United States. However, the events of the 1960s were to force many Americans—and not a few intellectuals—to examine the consequences of their actions, and to confront the close relationship between popular culture and cultural authority, and between such institutions as the university and the state.

3

WRITING THE WAR

> If at the end of a war story you feel uplifted, or if
> you feel some small bit of rectitude has been sal-
> vaged from the larger waste, then you have been
> made the victim of a very old and terrible lie.
>
> TIM O'BRIEN, "HOW TO TELL A WAR STORY,"
> IN *THE THINGS THEY CARRIED*

IN APPRAISING the writing of the war in Vietnam, one might be tempted to focus exclusively on the work
of academics and intellectuals, particularly those who have
written the histories that now constitute the official cultural
and political map of the era. Although I sketch a brief history
of the crucial roles that intellectuals played in assisting—and
resisting—the war in Vietnam, I consider in this chapter a selection of the unofficial (although not necessarily unpopular)
writing of the war that has come to inform another version of
its actualities, historical roots, and domestic consequences.
For rather than remain focused on the work produced by intellectuals (on which there has been much commentary), I
analyze some of the writings of Vietnam veterans, journalists,
and various unincorporated writers. Many of the authors who
have written for a popular audience about Vietnam stand in a
different relationship than professional intellectuals to the
processes of ideological mediation that have come to structure
the conventional understanding of the war. Indeed, much of
the Vietnam War writing that I will explore here offers an ex-
tensive critique of popular culture and war mythology, and
hence a very different understanding of history, knowledge,

and experience. This is not to imply an oppositional relationship between intellectuals and veterans, or theory and experience, because in the last analysis both intellectual and novelistic accounts are permeated by personal memory and official history.

The intellectual debates over the conduct of the war in Vietnam, and over the war's subsequent and various historical interpretations, have in many ways set the parameters of the discourse of the war itself. Those who have attempted to write the war from an alternative vantage point, whether from a desire to articulate personal experience or from a need to explore creatively the emergent identities and realities forged by Vietnam, often disclose a social and cultural terrain over which the end products of intellectual work (ideology posing as common sense) have only a tenuous influence. Rather than stand outside the ideological structures and constraints that intellectual work produces, such authors offer alternative and critical relationships to the realm of the popular wherein ideology continually strives to gain cultural purchase.

At least one of the results of intellectual work on the war has been the production of an ideological paradigm within which much of the present-day media debate over Vietnam is conducted. That paradigm is constituted by at least four major themes. First, and most importantly, is the claim that no one is to blame for the "quagmire" of the Vietnam War—neither the war planners and managers nor the military strategists and diplomats, and certainly not the politicians. It was a "tragedy without villains" that resulted from a "politics of inadvertence."[1] That claim leads to a second theme. Because blame cannot be fixed anywhere in particular, it follows that the war was a mystery that happened in a place and a time that no one will ever fully understand. The war is beyond knowledge and judicial investigation. Finally, and most pervasively, it is now argued that the war must be understood through the joining of the two remaining themes. On the one hand, "Vietnam was a war nobody won" because it was "a struggle between victims," with Americans and Vietnamese suffering equally.[2] On the other hand, nobody lost: the American military was never defeated on the battlefield, even though it failed, ultimately, to win the war.[3]

The roots of these ideological tropes were already visible during the 1960s as various government insiders began to publish their versions of the events that lead to the war in Vietnam.[4] During this period the influential part played by intellectuals in the planning and management of the Vietnam War became the subject of intense battles. Much of the conflict was conducted between various intellectual factions—both within and outside of government circles—but it also included a wider debate that tapped deep-seated anxieties about the nature and function of the intellectual in modern life. At one level, the controversy responded to an old set of questions that had gained new urgency in the 1960s—questions concerning the moral and political responsibilities of intellectuals, and the related problem of the proper relationship between intellectual work and the state. At another level, the 1960s witnessed the reemergence of a more widespread concern about the professionalization of all forms of knowledge, and the power and authority that experts and technicians had come to hold in society. Every aspect of modern life and death appeared to have attracted its particular regime of intellectuals and technocrats: from the workplace to the home, from child rearing to nutrition, from recreation to combat in Vietnam. Not surprisingly, in a world that had grown increasingly complex and over which a bewildering and often terrifying technology appeared to reign supreme, many people came to sympathize with the counterculture's antimodernist critique of the new American technocracy.[5]

One of the more lasting results of that interrogation of the moral responsibilities of intellectuals and of their participation in war management was a further fragmentation of intellectual discourse in the United States. Of course, intellectual life has always been prone to conflicts and epistemological breaks, especially during periods of rapid economic and cultural change. In times of war, moreover, not only are such transformations accelerated, but intellectuals are also more forcibly subjected to the pressures of patriotic persuasion, as well as to the more direct interventions of the state's apparatus of selectivity and ideological control.

To be sure, some intellectuals have often needed little in the way of prodding from governments—as the history of American intellectuals' involvement in the world wars and the Cold War demonstrate—and have been only too willing to put their knowledge and "cultural capital" at the service of the state. During World War I, for example, Randolph Bourne, whose writing would be "rediscovered" in the 1960s, was almost alone among his generation of intellectuals in refusing to capitulate to the official war line. In words that would later strike the Vietnam generation as prophetic, Bourne described the intellectuals of 1917 as "trained up in the pragmatic dispensation, immensely ready for the executive ordering of events, pitifully unprepared for the intellectual interpretation or the idealistic focusing of ends." In words that foreshadowed the later critique of the Cold War intellectuals during the Vietnam years, Bourne found his own generation eagerly lining up to make "themselves efficient instruments of the war technique, accepting with little question the ends as announced from above." Interestingly enough, Bourne also identified the college campuses as the primary site for the production of a certain kind of amoral pragmatism, or forms of instrumental reasoning detached from ethical considerations—in short, a mind set that is necessary for thinking and acting out the "war technique."⁶

Most certainly, the rise of McCarthyism following World War II, as well as the part that intellectuals and the universities played in legitimizing the Cold War hegemony that emerged within that gloomy period, helped to set the stage for a renewed period of critical debate over the relation between intellectuals and the state. The intensity of the intellectual controversies that erupted in the 1960s stemmed from the realization that intellectuals had played a central role in preparing American power for interventions in post-colonial struggles such as those in Vietnam. But the desire to act critically on the basis of that realization was due in large part to the pressures that had built up during the Cold War, when loyalty investigations, blacklisting, and anti-Communist witch-hunts devastated oppositional intellectuals and created in its wake a general retreat from politics. Disillusionment and conformity marked the age for those intellectuals of the left, leaving Irving Howe to characterize it as a time when "a whole generation was denied existence."[7]

The Cold War, however, was also a period when many intellectuals were being vigorously recruited by the state. At one level, that recruitment reflected the growing technical requirements of the emergent national security state (with its accompanying "military-industrial complex"), which not only drew intellectual workers into corporate and government research institutions but also brought the universities firmly under the sway of government funding and control. At another level, intellectuals were enlisted in the task of marking out the domestic ideological parameters of the Cold War, under the banner of "liberal pluralism," as well as engaging in the rationalization of new forms of state intervention in a whole range of social, cultural, and global activities.[8] Thus, by the beginning of the 1960s, power and knowledge had been brought into a new relationship with the state, and as the Vietnam War began to escalate in the Kennedy years, intellectuals were, in Bourne's words, operating as "efficient instruments of the war technique . . . as if the war and they had been waiting for each other."[9]

What Bourne identified in the early years of the century, and what the Cold War and Vietnam War would bring into sharp focus, was the historical process through which intellectual work was increasingly incorporated—in both enabling and problematic ways—into the structures of state power. The French theorist Julian Benda deplored the results of this process as early as the 1920s and suggested, with his by-now-classic phrase "la trahison des clercs," that intellectuals were no longer functioning as critically independent thinkers, but were acting to manipulate knowledge on behalf of political interests.[10] Elaborations of his critique underline how intellectuals faced two incompatible modes of functioning in society: the choice of "being the mouthpiece of power . . . or staying critically independent."[11] The traditional ideal of the intellectual as an individual who sought after universal truths and defended the free flow of ideas from a position of value-free disinterestedness had split into seemingly incompatible functions. What the Cold War demonstrated, and what the Vietnam War brought forcefully home to a new generation, was that many intellectuals were far from morally or politically disinterested; in fact, they represented a permanent "new class" based on its own self-interest.

But here was not a class in the traditional Marxist sense—a social stratum defined by specific economic interests and a relational status to the dominant mode of production—but an internally differentiated class interest "encompassing both technical intelligentsia and intellectuals" that shared a common experience of specialized training in the institutions of higher education.[12] The influence of that class stemmed from its ownership of cultural capital rather than its economic collateral—an accumulation of power rooted in historical shifts that have, since the Enlightenment, witnessed the rise of increasingly rational and secular modes of knowledge production. That rise in turn tended to produce more narrowly focused and specialized forms of knowledge, which were codified in the professional and institutional structures of specific knowledge regimes. Thus one of the central factors in the development of modern societies has been the entrance of intellectuals into the social arena as a significant cultural and political force. And although it is perhaps impossible to identify a specific form of shared ideology that defines all intellectuals as a class, powerful groups of intellectuals not only appear to share a paradigmatic desire for power but also exhibit an ability to reproduce themselves on the basis of theoretical and technical knowledge.[13]

What was demonstrated during the early 1960s, then, was

not particularly a new kind of situation for intellectuals, but a sudden expansion of a process that had been set in motion since at least the beginning of the Industrial Revolution. What was distinct about the Kennedy years was the sheer number of intellectuals who were welcomed into the administrative and planning agencies of the state or who willing proselytized on the state's behalf.[14] What the Vietnam War would then force with a vengeance to the center of intellectual life in the United States was the question of the moral and political responsibilities of intellectuals, as well as the related question of the proper relationship between intellectual work and the state. In the heated atmosphere of the 1960s such questions ultimately split professional intellectuals into warring camps. That fragmenting effect is easily identified at the institutional level of the universities, as I have noted, where, according to studies done by Everett Carll Ladd and Seymour Lipsett, the "agenda of academic politics had been substantially redrawn between 1969 and 1972."[15] For example, within such local affiliations as the "New York intellectuals," opinions on Vietnam and the social conflicts engendered by the war became so bitter that divisions emerged that have never closed. The difficulty for such intellectual groups was due in part to many of their members, radicals themselves during the 1930s, having since become intimately involved in creating the postwar "liberal consensus." As Alexander Bloom explains, the New York intellectuals had helped "articulate the belief that ideology had ended, and felt themselves growing closer to the centers of power in American society, as intellectual arbiters or, more directly, through visits and jobs in Washington." Moreover, the universities in postwar America had come to provide them with a prominent place in the Cold War order that seemed secure and relatively stable. But when that cozy social order became the object of intense criticism, Bloom points out, "their position became increasingly problematic . . . they were caught between their prewar inclinations and their postwar beliefs and places."[16] For some, such as Dwight MacDonald, Mary McCarthy, William Phillips, and Philip

Rahv, the rise of the antiwar movement and the New Left reawakened a radical spirit that had been prudently mothballed during the excesses of the Cold War. A few younger intellectuals, those like Susan Sontag, Norman Mailer, and Leslie Fiedler, became associated with New Left politics and were active participants in a number of social and antiwar protests. Many others, however, either bunkered down for the duration (Lionel Trilling, for example)[17] or took a variety of positions in opposition to the new social radicalism (Irving Howe, Nathan Glazer, Seymour Lipsett, Daniel Bell, Irving Kristol, and others). In the case of Norman Podhoretz, the editor of *Commentary*, the impact of the 1960s set in motion a quite complex trajectory. In the late 1950s and early 1960s Podhoretz had been a critic of the Cold War intellectuals and was openly calling for a renewal of radical activism. Following the Berkeley "Free Speech" demonstrations of 1964, however, he suddenly cooled on the activists and began to support a more conservative line. Nevertheless, in 1971 he was demanding the immediate withdrawal of American forces from Vietnam. Later in the 1970s Podhoretz would emerge as an outspoken organizer of the neoconservative backlash against sixties radicalism and its lingering influence. This kind of movement across the 1960s was not unusual and represents yet another index to the shifts taking place around intellectual work in the wake of the war.

Nevertheless, many intellectuals during the Vietnam War era continued to maintain the existing weave of ideology and knowledge, and to create a sense of continuity in the face of shifting political priorities and demands. To borrow from Gramsci, each new phase in the development of hegemony blocs creates "one or more strata of intellectuals which give it homogeneity and an awareness of its own function not only in the economic but also in the social and political fields . . . the industrial technician, the specialist in political economy, the organizers of a new culture, of a new legal system."[18] Brief as Kennedy's presidency was, his administration was able to generate a sense of enthusiasm and optimism among intellectuals. Consequently, "the sense of connection to power" was genuinely felt throughout the variegated strata of intellectual life in the United States. Under Kennedy, wrote Hannah Arendt, intellectuals came to enjoy a new status and to feel that they were now "somebodies and not nobodies."[19] Thus the historical process through which intellectual work was incorporated into government and corporate bureaucracies reached new heights during the early 1960s, and for the most part, intellectuals became enthusiastic insiders and ideologues of the "New Frontier." By the middle of the decade, however, the war in Vietnam would embroil that new frontier spirit in bitter controversies that would fragment intellectual communities and bring the institutions of higher education to the brink of collapse.

To reiterate an earlier point: it is not that intellectuals' attraction to power marked something new in American culture and politics; rather, the sheer number of intellectuals who were welcomed into the Kennedy administration, or who willingly proselytized on its behalf, seemed to inaugurate a new age in which the "cultural capital" of intellectuals was suddenly inflated by the pressures of demand. When the Vietnam War began to shift the national consciousness in other directions, the ideology of the intellectual's function in culture as either disinterested technician or scholar came to strike many as hypocritical and false. Far from being disinterested, it now seemed disturbingly clear that this "new class" of professional intellectuals was responsible, in large part, for the creation and execution of American foreign and military policy in Vietnam. That realization struck oppositional intellectuals such as Noam Chomsky as a frightening testament to the self-interested, instrumental, and amoral concepts of humanity and civilization that intellectuals were bringing to the exercise of power. With American technology and personnel "running amuck in Southeast Asia," Chomsky was to write, many intellectuals "can be counted on . . . to provide the ideological justification for this particular form of barbarism and to decry the irresponsibility and lack of sophistication of those who will find all of this intolerable and revolting."[20] By the latter half of the 1960s many American citizens had also come to view the war in Vietnam as intolerable and revolting, and Chomsky's view was shared even by some of those intellectuals who worked within the government, and by those who might normally be expected to support its policies.

Symptomatic in this regard is the case of Daniel Ellsberg, a Harvard-educated State Department insider who had been deeply involved in many of the planning aspects of the Vietnam War. His growing disgust with the war, however, eventually pushed him into making public the Pentagon Papers, a history of the intellectual and political decision-making process behind America's conduct of the war in Vietnam. Published by the *New York Times* in 1971, the Pentagon Papers tended to confirm what New Left critics of the war had been saying for years, namely, that successive administrations had deliberately misled the American people about their real intentions in Vietnam.

On another level, Ellsberg's evolution from hawk to dove is revealing of a more general shift of consciousness within the public sphere of the 1960s. Throughout the late 1950s and 1960s, Ellsberg was a privileged figure in government war planning in general and, later, on the subject of Vietnam in particular. He began his career as a strategic analyst with the Rand Corporation, the California-based think tank for the Air Force, where he was privy to the nation's most secret nuclear warfare planning documents. Following Kennedy's election in 1960, Ellsberg moved to Washington, where he became one of the many intellectuals whose expertise was suddenly in demand at the very center of national power and decision making.

America's growing involvement in Vietnam attracted Ellsberg's attention, and following Johnson's escalation of the war in 1964, he managed to get himself assigned to Edward G. Lansdale's special State Department team operating in Vietnam. Lansdale had been running covert operations in Vietnam since the mid-1950s and was something of a legendary figure to younger agents like Ellsberg. However, Ellsberg spent a good deal of his time in Vietnam with John Paul

Vann, a maverick special forces advisor and later civilian-military advisor. Vann's theories about how the United States ought to be fighting the war in Vietnam ran almost completely counter to the tactics thought up by Pentagon intellectuals, adopted by the general staff, and put into practice by General Westmoreland. Vann's thesis was, in short, that the war could not be won by military power alone; there had to be a complimentary and integrated social program of reforms capable of convincing ordinary Vietnamese that a decent and secure future lay with the U.S.-supported non-Communist forces. Westmoreland's search-and-destroy tactics, which relied heavily on the often indiscriminate and destructive violence of artillery and air power, combined with continued U.S. support for the various corrupt and unpopular regimes in Saigon, seemed almost custom designed to alienate the majority of Vietnamese citizens. Ellsberg agreed with Vann's assessment but, having witnessed firsthand the often aimless violence of the American way of war in Vietnam, ultimately came to the conclusion that the war had become irreversibly stalemated and that no one's interests were being served by America's continuing presence in the country.[21]

Returning to the United States in 1967, Ellsberg worked for Secretary of Defense Robert McNamara compiling the forty-three-volume study that would become known as the Pentagon Papers. The decision to go public with the papers was an irrevocable one for Ellsberg—it resulted in an immediate shift in his status, demoting him from privileged insider to political outsider, and subsequently marked him as a target in a campaign organized specifically to discredit him.[22]

The way Ellsberg describes the shift in his life—from what I have called, following Raymond Williams, "lived ideology" to "critical knowledge"—provides us with a model for understanding the levels of consciousness through which many Americans passed during the 1960s and early 1970s. Ellsberg writes of his evolution from insider to activist as a movement in three stages. First, he viewed America's involvement in Vietnam as a problem that he wished to help solve; then he came to see the conflict as a stalemate, from which America needed to extract itself with as much honor as possible; and finally, he arrived at the conclusion that the war was a "crime . . . a brutal fraud, a lawless imperial adventure" that had to be exposed and resisted at all costs.[23]

The intellectual process and timing of Ellsberg's transition from insider to outsider was, like Podhoretz's opposite trajectory, not unique. For example, by the late 1960s, Walter Lippmann, the perennial political commentator and presidential advisor since the administration of Woodrow Wilson, found himself in the unlikely position of political outcast, alienated from Washington's inner circles as a result of his increasingly vitriolic opposition to President Johnson's escalation of the Vietnam War. In the early 1960s Lippmann had supported American policy in Vietnam, writing that he could see no alternative to sticking with the South Vietnamese government led by Ngo Dinh Diem.[24] For many intellectuals, including Lippmann and Ellsberg, that stage of America's involvement was viewed as a matter of problem solving that the United States had inherited from World War II. Then, in 1963, Diem was assassinated in a military coup after months of unrest had demonstrated the fundamental unpopularity of his regime. For the next four years, as American involvement steadily increased, Vietnam was to suffer a series of coups and countercoups until General Nguyen Van Thieu would emerge as president in 1967. By that time the United States would have committed half a million troops, and the bombing of both North and South Vietnam would be in full swing. In 1965 Lippmann reached the conclusion that the only way to unlock the increasingly violent stalemate in Vietnam was to negotiate a speedy withdrawal. He would write that although the "warhawks would rejoice" over a full-scale war in Asia, the "people would weep before it ended" and that the only honorable solution was a negotiated peace.[25] By the summer of 1967, however, Lippmann had moved from his usual measured critical stance to become implacably opposed to the war and to the Johnson administration's conduct of it. Deploying what a recent biographer terms "a new vocabulary," one that describes the president as consumed by a "messianic megalomania," Lippmann was to express his dissent thus: "There is a growing belief that Johnson's America is no longer the historic America, that it is a bastard empire which relies on superior force to achieve its purpose, and is no longer an example of the wisdom and humanity of a free society. . . . It is a feeling that the American promise has been betrayed and abandoned."[26]

Lippmann was not the only dissenting voice from the older generation of American thinkers to express feelings of alienation and betrayal. Archibald MacLeish, for example, "long recognized as something of an unofficial minister of culture," declared that Vietnam "raised the question of whether the nation had become indifferent to the opinions of mankind and outgrown its old idealism."[27] Similarly, Lewis Mumford, in his presidential address to the American Academy of Arts and Letters, expressed "anger" and "shame" at the United States' policies in Vietnam and called upon all those who were "devoted to the pursuit of the arts and humane letters" to "speak out openly in protest on every occasion when human beings are threatened by arbitrary power." Those human beings include not only oppressed blacks in the South, he argued, but also "the peoples of both North and South Vietnam who must now confront our government's cold blooded blackmail and calculated violence." Mumford further speculated, as did many others in the 1960s, whether the United States was not in fact doing more to promote totalitarianism and corrupt legitimate governments than its Cold War opponent, the Soviet Union.[28]

These three latter examples of established figures speaking out against the war indicate the war's eroding effects on the post–World War II ideological paradigm. On a more general level, the widening gulf between the government and sections of the intelligentsia was clearly signaled in the spring of 1965. In March of that year the first mass "teach-in" against the war, aimed at countering government propaganda, was held at the University of Michigan, a practice that spread rapidly to other campuses across the nation. In May the first "national teach-in" was held in Washington, D.C., an event that was extensively covered by the media. The *New York Times* printed a complete transcript of the proceedings, which it referred to as "the most significant gathering of intellectuals since the Constitutional Convention."[29]

If the teach-ins were exercises in mass education aimed at countering establishment propaganda, the summer of 1965 offered many intellectuals and artists an opportunity to make a more personal gesture of opposition to President Johnson's foreign policy. That opportunity came during the White House Festival of the Arts. The festival was conceived by Johnson's advisor on intellectual affairs, the historian Eric Goldman, as an opportunity to bring together the nation's foremost intellectuals, artists, and patrons of the arts. In the event, however, the festival became a platform for intellectual dissent as well as a litmus test of individual positions on the war. Among the first to make a stand was the poet Robert Lowell, who wrote to the president saying that he felt "conscious bound" to refuse the invitation on the grounds that he did not want to be associated with an administration whose foreign policy he viewed "with the greatest dismay and distrust."[30] Lowell released his letter to the press, where it generated a good deal of debate among intellectuals. One result was the arrival at the White House of a telegram in support of Lowell's stand, signed by an impressive cross-section of artists and intellectuals that included Hannah Arendt, Jules Feiffer, Lillian Hellman, Alfred Kazin, Dwight Mac-Donald, Philip Roth, Mark Rothko, William Styron, Robert Penn Warren, and others.[31] The telegram was also released to the press, where once again it generated much interest and debate. As might be expected, the festival itself was a tense affair (a petition against the war was circulated among the guests, for example) that drove President Johnson to exclaim before the press: "Some of them insult me by staying away and some of them insult me by coming."[32]

The 1960s, having begun with a sense of opening new frontiers in which government institutions and intellectuals would create new ways of defining the "American Century," thus drew to a close with government officials and intellectuals locked in an acrimonious debate. Indeed, the relationship between the government and the intellectual community grew increasingly strained throughout the rest of the decade and into the Nixon years of the early 1970s.[33] Borrowing terms from Gramsci again, it is possible to say that sections of the intellectual community had ceased to perform their traditional function as the legitimizers of the state and as the elaborators of hegemonic imperatives. In this sense, incorporated "organic" intellectuals like Ellsberg, who had risen with the Cold War hegemonic system, and "traditional" intellectuals such as Lippman, who represented a continuity of legitimacy between historical hegemonic blocs, were forced by events to shift their affiliations to the emergent and unincorporated organic intellectuals of the antiwar movement.

In the case of, for example, the New Left, perhaps the major emergent intellectual sensibility of the 1960s, the desire to resist and expose the ideological functioning of the state was immediately manifest.[34] But as we have seen in the case of Ellsberg and Lippmann, the movement toward resistance often entailed a painful process of discarding achieved status and peeling away residual prejudices and assumptions. The point is that the Vietnam War provoked deeply felt passions and anxieties, not national solidarity, and these involved the entire national identity in all of its symbolic, ideological, and representational forms. In that sense, it was indeed impossible to win the war, because neither Johnson nor Nixon controlled the language of war (as did Roosevelt or Churchill, for example, during World War II). The longer the war dragged on, the more the cultural discourse of war (patriotism, heroism, self-sacrifice, and so on) grew threadbare and meaningless.

As the philosopher of the politics of war Carl von Clausewitz has written, war may well generate its own grammar, but its speech, its writing, and its logic are entirely a product of the domestic cultures of political discourse.[35] By the late 1960s, intellectuals—for whom meaning and language and its

supplement, writing, are the primary means of production—
were deeply divided over the Vietnam War, and many felt
alienated from the political discourse that attempted to support and legitimize it. There thus developed a conflict-ridden
politics of meaning and interpretation that continues to have
effects in the present—not the least of which involves the
relationship between the Vietnam War and popular culture,
a relationship that is perhaps most compellingly revealed
in the writings of Vietnam veterans, journalists, and other
writers.

Popular culture is where the war came from, so to speak,
in the sense that it is where political and social identities are
constructed and valorized for the vast majority of people—
it is where culture, in all of its complex tangles of residual,
dominant, and emergent forms, overlaps with and is en-
folded back into structures of authority and control. What is
demonstrated most vividly in much of the popular writing
on the war, and what is most often elided in the writings of
intellectuals, is precisely that relationship. Intellectual work
often involves self-effacement and theoretical distancing from
issues and problems. Moreover, because a good deal of that
kind of writing reproduced variations on the "quagmire thesis," insisting on the "tragedy without villains" approach, the
actual material and subjective consequences of intellectual
and political production went unaddressed. As much as intellectual writing gives us broad overviews of the "events" of
the era, it often tells us little about more-localized experiences where the conflicts and contradictions of official policies are lived out at the level of everyday life. In order to gain
access to this region of experience, it is therefore useful to
turn to the various "unofficial" accounts of the Vietnam War,
where the mystifying effects of popular culture, politics, and
intellectual work are interrogated and at least temporarily
called into question.

In the memoirs and novels that have emerged from Vietnam we find an extremely subjective and altogether more
painful sense of lived experience than evidenced in much
intellectual writing of the war. Here, the theoretical strategies

of intellectual self-effacement are turned inside out, and what emerges is a personal immersion into the emotional and psychological terrain of history and popular memory. That terrain exposes a traumatic sense of cultural identities in crisis—male identities, for the most part, that have been left decentered and precarious by the defeat in Vietnam. Investigations of the cultural constituents of selfhood abound in this literature, and in the process, the outlines of a critical historical paradigm emerges. That this paradigm is permeated with an intensely bitter cynicism should come as no surprise, given that, as Peter Sloterdijk has so persuasively argued, cynical reasoning represents the most pervasive social and psychic legacy of the 1960s. Sloterdijk's claim is that contemporary subjectivity is structured by what he calls "enlightened false consciousness," the ability to know and yet constantly distract oneself from the troubling fact of having been duped.[36] That warped sense of self-knowledge is what informs the corrosive apathy and amnesia that signify the dominant mode of being in the aftermath of the Vietnam era.

What much of the Vietnam writing grapples with at the level of personal memory, then, is the ways in which the modern subject of popular culture comes to be constructed as the future subject of war. Specifically, such writings attempt to show how social identities were constructed in the militarized culture of the Cold War, and how those identities proved ultimately unstable under the dual ideological assault of the war in Vietnam and the war at home. There is, then, a rejection of those contrivances that would displace war and death onto historical myths of a politics of inadvertence, or that condense two decades of killing and maiming into the metaphor of the quagmire. That rejection is not a simple matter of writing more honest or truthful accounts of the Vietnam era, however; it is instead a matter of insisting on examining the ways in which subjectivities inhabit, and are inhabited by, popular culture, and how certain kinds of critiques illuminate the connections otherwise left opaque and obscure.

MEMORY, HISTORY, AND THE LITERARY PROCESS

Some of the most dramatic moments in the struggle over the meaning of the Vietnam War were enacted between 1965 and 1972. Afterward, what had been a stirring public debate seemingly splintered into a multitude of private anxieties and personal agonizing. As I noted in chapter 1, Peter Marin locates part of the blame for the cultural malaise that set in during the post–Vietnam War years in the war's literary history. There he found a general refusal "to confront, directly, the realities of the war, or to have considered it, at least in part, from the Vietnamese point of view—in terms of their suffering rather than ours."[37] Although Marin is correct, as far as he goes, I suggested that the history of the reception of Graham Greene's novel *The Quiet American* complicates Marin's model of literary production and consumption, and that the novel itself refutes his claim that the writing on the war is solely concentrated on American problems. Of course, Greene is not an American, and he was not writing, as many veterans of the war write, from within a fractured sense of selfhood that resulted from his experiences in Vietnam. Nevertheless, the conflicting critical responses to *The Quiet American* constitute an early example of the shifting ideological patterns that have structured the cultural possibilities of the war's reception in America.

A more contemporary example of that process of selection and reception can be identified with David Halberstam's *One Very Hot Day* (1968). Halberstam's novel, like Greene's, fulfills Marin's demand that novelists engage with the moral questions raised by the Vietnam War within the context of both Vietnamese and American sensibilities. Also like Greene's novel, *One Very Hot Day* initially failed to find a popular audience, even though it was generally well received by the critics. Indeed, *One Very Hot Day* was quickly bought up and serialized by the *Saturday Evening Post*; the Literary Guild chose it as their selection of the month; and the *New York Times Book Review* ran a positive front-page review. Thus the novel's failure to find a popular audience in the spring of

1968 came as a surprise to Halberstam, leaving him to speculate whether he, like Lyndon Johnson, "had simply been
overtaken by events."[38] This was, after all, the period of the
Tet Offensive, an event that shattered any lingering illusions
of a quick victory in Vietnam and irreversibly shifted national consciousness dramatically against the war. Consequently, *One Very Hot Day* soon went out of print and was
unavailable for more than a decade, only to reemerge again
in the more receptive conditions of the 1980s.

One Very Hot Day deals with the early, or Kennedy, phase
of the Vietnam War, when the conflict was a relatively small
affair of elite "advisors" and "special forces." The irregular or
counterinsurgency aspect of the war in Vietnam had already
proven popular with Roger Moore's best-seller *The Green
Berets* (1965). But whereas Moore portrays the special forces
and their operations as a heroic and righteous crusade against
communism in an attempt to mythologize the American
cause in Vietnam, Halberstam's novel offers a vision of fatigue
and of inevitable defeat. The main conduits for this sensibility are Captain Beaupre, a cynical and out-of-shape veteran
of the Korean War, and Lieutenant Thuong, a Vietnamese
soldier who has lived through the French defeat in Vietnam
and who has come to conclude that the Americans, too, will
fail. From their contrasting historical and cultural perspectives, Beaupre and Thuong reach similar conclusions.

The novel is structured around a single day's patrol in the
sweltering heat of Vietnam's Mekong Delta region. For Beaupre, this patrol, like all the others before it, is a waste of
time—a long and dangerous walk that achieves nothing. Not
only are the Viet Cong so well integrated into the local village
system that it is impossible to tell friend from foe, but the
South Vietnamese soldiers are also simply not interested in
risking their lives for abstract objectives. Moreover, Beaupre
finds the fundamental nature of this new kind of warfare
alienating:

it was not just helicopters . . . it was everything new about this
war; helicopters, spotter dogs which were guaranteed to find VC

but were driven insane by the heat and bit Americans instead,
water purification people, psywar people, civilians in military
clothes, military in civilian clothes, words which said one thing
and always meant another . . . (73)

Those thoughts are picked up again later in the novel as
Beaupre compares the straightforwardness of his previous
war experience with that in Vietnam:

> here you began with distrust, you assumed it about everything,
> even things you thought you knew. Even the Americans seemed
> different to him now, and he trusted them less; in order to survive
> in this new world and this new Army, they had changed. Yes was
> no longer exactly yes, no was no longer exactly no, maybe was
> more certainly maybe. (133)

Not only does he come to mistrust his own people, but he
also realizes that this war of endless patrols—walking in "a
goddamn circle" (119) just as the French had before them—is
strategically designed to accomplish little except the meaningless killing of unwilling Vietnamese conscripts and villagers. In spite of the realities in the field, the war generates
an official language of its own, which does not relate to
actual conditions and which, in fact, works deliberately to
obscure the actualities of those conditions. Thus Beaupre
comes to liken this new American army to "bloodsuckers"
who have "read all their own publicity and . . . got themselves sure as hell brainwashed, and they see themselves not
as bloodsuckers, not that at all, but as lifesavers" (146). Rather
like Greene's portrayal of Alden Pyle's morally drained and
disconnected approach to conditions in Vietnam, Halberstam describes a military mind-set that is also incapable of
grasping the real historical and cultural dynamics of the
country in which the American soldiers must fight.

Beaupre's sense that the war is an absurd mess that the
Americans are destined to lose is reflected in the thoughts of
Thuong, who has observed the Americans with "a mounting
sense of disappointment" (46). When the Americans had first
arrived, he had hoped that they would "change what no one
else could change":

they did not, after all, lose wars, that was very well known in all the history books (even the French ones) and they were big and rich (much richer, he knew, than the French) and somehow they would bring the touch for this to Vietnam . . . and then suddenly one day he had realized what was really happening, that instead of changing Vietnam, they were changing with it, and becoming part of it; until finally he was more aware of their frailties than he was of Vietnamese frailties. (46–47)

Instead of changing the endless cycle of lies that marked the South Vietnamese government's approach to the war, the Americans are becoming eager participants in the corruption. For Thuong, the unending conflict is a downward spiral in which a few become rich and powerful, while the majority grow increasingly angry: "Everywhere we go now, everyone is angrier. We are angrier . . . the enemy is angrier and the people are angrier. It gets worse every day" (46). Like Beaupre, Thuong realizes that the war is being lost, and the more he experiences the fatalism and frustration of the war, the more he "envied the Communists their self-belief, their ideology, their certainty . . . the passion and commitment their life took" (138). There is no sense of passion for the cause among Thuong's comrades or superiors, and consequently the language of the war is not about real objectives or goals— it merely signifies the day-to-day needs of survival:

in this country what was the truth any more, could you find it, and if you did, did it matter? You told the truth and you were killed for it, you lied and hid the truth and perhaps you survived; the truth was a terrible luxury. A man wanted to live, that was the truth . . . and anything he said was designed not for honor but simply to gain the next day. (80)

One Very Hot Day and The Quiet American are examples of critical fictions that, in different historical moments and for different reasons, failed to find a large reading public. The Quiet American was beyond the ideological pale, so to speak, and politically unacceptable in the Cold War culture of the 1950s. One Very Hot Day, on the other hand, appeared at the height of the antiwar agitation and at a time when the images of Vietnam combat were a nightly television event. Halberstam's novel is not, however, the only example of Vietnam War fiction that did not do well in that period. Indeed, no Vietnam War novel did well between the late 1960s and the latter half of the 1970s.[39] Furthermore, those few authors who did manage to get into print consistently met difficulties finding a publisher willing to deal with Vietnam material. For example, James Webb, author of *Fields of Fire* (1978), claims to have been turned down by nine publishers before his manuscript was accepted, and the Vietnam war poet William Ehrhart reports that it took him ten years to find a publisher for his work.[40] According to publisher Jervis Jurjevics, those experiences were not unusual. He recalls sitting "in editorial boards and marketing meetings turning down novel after novel" on the Vietnam War.[41] Moreover, even when a manuscript did make it through the publishing process, it still had to face generally hostile reviewers. For example, William Pelfrey's *The Big V* (1972) was called "obscene" by a reviewer in the *Library Journal*.[42] Writing in the *New Republic* in 1978, Zalin Grant claims that in the first half of the 1970s "critics seemed all too ready to shut off any further discussion of the war."[43] In particular, Grant notes that in the spring of 1974, reviewers in both the *New York Times Book Review* and *Time* magazine were insisting that the public "does not want to hear any more about Viet Nam":

> The country was undeniably war-weary, the ceasefire had been signed the year before. Still, this negative attitude toward the publication of Vietnam books by two of the nation's most powerful organs—whose prophecies have a way of becoming self-fulfilling—was close to being an act of censorship. The ripple effect was immediately noticeable in the attitude of other reviewers across the country. How many manuscripts of merit, we shall never know, were later turned down by publishers because "the public doesn't want to hear about it."[44]

Apart from the institutional constraints that hampered the emergence of a Vietnam War literature, there also existed a number of other problems. For instance, a decade of almost nonstop conflict over Vietnam had undoubtedly created a desire to erase the whole experience from cultural memory. As we have seen, Peter Marin identifies this act of self-willed amnesia as a form of paralysis that kept Americans from examining, and therefore working through, a deeply felt sense of national guilt. But perhaps the single most compelling factor is one of finding a language capable of speaking the seemingly unspeakable—of speaking about an unpopular war that was also America's first military defeat.

At one level, here was a problem of confronting established myths that were no longer tenable in their original ideological form, and of forging new myths from among the determining possibilities of new kinds of knowledge in a context where the emergent ideologies of defeat had yet to be absorbed and solidified. Quite apart from the problems of writing the war, however, there was also, as I have noted, a whole range of cultural institutions that were working to marginalize the Vietnam experience. Even when some elements of this ideological gatekeeping and cultural selection could agree on the worthiness of a piece of Vietnam writing, the uncertainty of popular reception remained beyond the influence of the institutions of literary production. The struggle to establish a language of the Vietnam experience, then, came to pass within a contested process in which the possibilities and difficulties of literary production and reception formed part of a wider range of cultural negotiations taking place in the aftermath of Vietnam.

That a literature of the Vietnam War has now established itself as a popular and profitable form of textual practice is perhaps an indication of how central the Vietnam War has been to so many lives. In spite of attempts to ignore, repress, or distort the experience of Vietnam, a receptive readership ultimately emerged, showing all the signs of a collective consciousness that was in need of expression. While politicians and official intellectuals were insisting during the 1970s on the need to "turn the page" and "move on" from the experience of Vietnam, it is now clear that a large audience existed that wanted access to what was in danger of becoming a historically unavailable event. That the literary language of the Vietnam War often turned out to be experimental in form, and in any case far removed from the literary heroics of previous wars, again speaks to a popular desire to know about the war in ways that had not been tended to by other media. In literary terms far removed from the narrative strategies of political insiders and historians, much of the initial writing by veterans was decidedly angry, personal, and aimed at deconstructing the popular American myths of war. Unlike most intellectual writing, which generally situates its concerns outside the realm of popular culture, some of the best Vietnam War novels sought to expose the subjective roots of war within popular culture and to insist upon its power to organize pleasures and desires in a moral economy of war.

One of the most forceful articulations of the new collective consciousness is to be found in Ron Kovic's *Born on the Fourth of July* (1976). Not only does Kovic's memoir represent an early example of the emergence of a popular language of the Vietnam experience, but it also found support from critics. Yet Kovic's narrative style does not proceed by the conventional cause-effect logic of classical realism. On the contrary, the temporal organization of *Born on the Fourth of July* moves back and forth across various emotional registers of experience and memory. The first chapter, which recounts the moment when Kovic is wounded and paralyzed in Vietnam, is narrated in an impressionistic first-person voice. The final chapter, which details the operation in which Kovic is shot, alternates between first- and third-person narration. Subsequent chapters, and especially those that explore the subjective anguish of coming to terms with paralysis, are narrated in the third person, while the section that describes the Marine boot camp training is recounted in a stream-of-consciousness style that is printed in alternating patterns of upper- and lowercase letters. These experimental devices create a style in stark contrast to the popular conventions of combat realism that have traditionally marked war writing. More importantly, Kovic also refuses to reconstruct the war experience as something that can be confined solely to Vietnam. Instead, Kovic sees himself as a victim of American culture and politics—a culture that constitutes its male subjects according to false ideals of heroism, and a political system that coldly sends young males off to fight and die in such places as Vietnam. Here, as in many other accounts by veterans, the fiery idealism of President Kennedy is recalled as a point of origin, a moment of emotional and moral commitment to the desires of the state. Kovic recalls the mass cultural preparation for that moment, a childhood spent absorbing the adventures of such television heroes as the Lone Ranger, Roy Rogers, and Captain Video. As Kovic explains, Saturday mornings were spent at the local cinema watching John Wayne and Audie Murphy war movies, and afterward, playing war games with toy guns in the local woods. Kovic also recounts his boyhood experiences as a Cub Scout, marching in Memorial Day parades and dreaming of becoming a high school sports hero. Then, almost inevitably, in his last month of school, the marine recruiters arrived and Kovic was convinced that there could be nothing finer than to be one of "the few good men," serving his country "like the young president had asked us to do."[45]

Kovic's experience of warfare in Vietnam, however, was anything but heroic. In what amounted to a period of unrelenting horror and confusion, Kovic participated in the senseless killing of women and children, and was himself responsible for the accidental shooting death of a fellow marine. Then, during his second tour of duty, this phase of his life came to a sudden and violent end when a Viet Cong bullet paralysed him from the chest down. Sent back to the United States, the horror and confusion merely continued as the ugly finality of his paralysis gradually sank in. To make matters worse, he was assigned to insensitive and indifferent treatment in an overcrowded and underfinanced Veterans Administration hospital, where on one occasion, after demanding better care from the staff, he was told by a nurse that "Vietnam don't mean nothin' to me . . . you can take your Vietnam and shove it up your ass" (131).

Through many such experiences, and through a process of self-education in the history of America's involvement in Vietnam, Kovic is gradually drawn to the antiwar movement. In the spring of 1970 he traveled with a friend to Washington, where he joined the demonstration against the invasion of Cambodia. At first he was unsure of his feelings toward the demonstration because much of it seemed "like a weird carnival." But there was also a sense of togetherness "just as there had been in Vietnam" among the soldiers. But this was a "togetherness of a different kind of people and for a much different reason." In Vietnam "we were killing and maiming people. In Washington on that Saturday afternoon in May we were trying to heal them and set them free" (140). Thus, when the police inevitably charged the ranks of the demonstrators and began arresting people, Kovic became enraged at the senseless use of violence. At a later demonstration where he was one of the speakers, Kovic was thrown from his wheelchair by police, beaten up, and arrested—an incident that convinced him that an official government policy existed that was determined to repress his experiences. He came to view himself as the living icon of misguided government policies in Vietnam, a "living reminder of something terrible and awful" that must be silenced:

he had been their Yankee Doodle Dandy, their all-American boy. He had given them almost his whole being in the war and now, after all that, they weren't satisfied with three-quarters being gone, they wanted to take the rest of him. . . . It had all been a dirty trick and he didn't know what to think anymore. . . . He had never been anything but a thing to them, a thing to put a uniform on and train to kill, a young thing to run through the meat-grinder, a cheap small nothing to make mincemeat out of. (166)

The politicians, the "small men with small ideas," had "gambled with his life and hustled him off to war" and consigned him to a "living death" (167).

Born on the Fourth of July is a powerful indictment of the militarized mass culture of the 1950s, which filled young men's minds with the mass-mediated fantasies of an always virtuous America—an America that emptied out politically into the myth-destroying terrain of Vietnam. Kovic concludes his story where he begins it, at that point where his former sense of selfhood came to a violent and irrevocable end when a bullet shattered his spine. All Kovic could feel in this moment was how he had been cheated out of life: "All I could feel was the worthlessness of dying, right here in this place at this moment for nothing" (222). Kovic's memoir ends with a sad two-line poem that sums up an entire generation's sense of anguished resignation in the face of the multitude of unanswered questions and failed dreams that mark the post-sixties mind-set: "It was all sort of easy / It had all come and gone" (224).

Another war veteran, Philip Caputo, reaches conclusions similar to Kovic's in *A Rumor of War* (1977), a memoir that deploys a more conventional realism than *Born on the Fourth of July.* Caputo's book also attempts to situate Vietnam within a larger literary history of warfare, beginning with the very title of his memoir, which is taken from the New Testament. Each chapter is introduced with a telling quote drawn from a range of texts, including the writings of Roman military historians, Shakespeare, Rudyard Kipling, and, most often, literary and poetic responses to World War I.

Part 1, for example, is entitled "The Splendid Little War," a title that invokes the jubilant response of then U.S. Secretary of State John Hay to the successful military campaign in the Philippines during the Spanish-American War of 1898. The war with Spain, it will be remembered, marked not only the entrance of the United States onto the world stage as a major military power, but it also served notice on the other imperial powers that America was now a power to be reckoned with in the division of Asian spoils. At the same time, however, Caputo is concerned in this section to evoke "something of the romantic flavor of Kipling's colonial wars," (63) suggesting the powerful influence of that particular form of romanticized imperial history on the minds of young boys who have yet to experience the horrors of war. The title of the final section, however, "In Death's Grey Land," taken from Siegfried Sassoon's World War I poetry, suggests the experiential distance traveled by Caputo and his generation. Like the "lost generation" of veteran writers of that earlier era, whose artistic sensibilities were wrenched into new modes of perception through the experience of trench warfare, Caputo feels that he, too, has been changed by the war and now experiences the world as an alienated cultural outsider.

Literary allusions aside, Caputo admits to having been seduced by the same mass cultural influences as Kovic—"a boyhood diet of war movies and blood-and-guts novels"— which left him ill-prepared for the actualities of war in Vietnam.[46] Like Kovic, the accumulated effects of mass culture made Caputo vulnerable to President Kennedy's stirring campaign rhetoric—a rhetoric that seemed designed to play upon the unworldly innocence of a generation brought up on war movies and TV adventure series. Caputo sums up that moment of his pre-Vietnam self:

> War is always attractive to young men who know nothing about it, but we had also been seduced into uniform by Kennedy's challenge to "ask what you can do for your country" and by the missionary idealism he had awakened in us. America seemed omnipotent then: the country could still claim it had never lost a war, and we believed we were ordained to play cop to the Communists' robber and spread our own faith around the world . . . we saw ourselves as the champions of a cause that was destined to triumph. (xiv)

Thus Caputo arrived in Vietnam with the unquestioned moral assumption that he was involved in a righteous mission. We "carried along with our packs and rifles," he writes, "the implicit convictions that the Viet Cong would be quickly beaten . . . that we were doing something altogether noble and good" (xiv). But in words that reveal the narrative trajectory of the book as a whole, Caputo adds that "we kept the packs and rifles; the convictions, we lost" (xiv). What is eventually made clear is that the disintegration of American ideological and cultural assumptions in Vietnam could, and often did, produce savagery among what had once been "good, solid kids." Caputo continues: "It was the dawn of creation in the Indochina bush, an ethical as well as a geographical wilderness. Out there, lacking restraints, sanctioned to kill, confronted by a hostile country and a relentless enemy, we sank into a brutish state" (xx).

Upon his return to the United States, Caputo, like Kovic, was drawn to the antiwar movement, although he admits to retaining "a strong attachment to Vietnam"—an attachment, however, that "did not spring from any patriotic ideas about duty, honor, and sacrifice, the myths with which old men send young men off to get killed and maimed" (xvi). Rather, it was the recognition that an irreversible change had been brought about by his Vietnam experience. "Though we were civilians again," Caputo writes, "the civilian world seemed alien. We did not belong to it as much as we did to that other world, where we had fought and our friends had died" (xvi). The deeply emotional experience of Vietnam had created two irreconcilable desires in Caputo: a loathing of the war's savagery, which ultimately drove him into the peace movement and the organization Vietnam Veterans against the War, and an intense nostalgia for the profound and selfless intimacy of comradeship that he had felt in Vietnam, and that kept him from hating the war with quite the intensity of fellow peace activists: "I could protest as loudly as the most convinced activist, but I could not deny the grip the war had on me, nor the fact that it had been an experience as fascinating as it was repulsive, as exhilarating as it was sad, as tender as it was cruel" (xvi).

Caputo's antiwar activism began while he was still serving in Vietnam, and grew out of an incident in which two Vietnamese villagers were murdered by soldiers under his command. The murders resulted from two related pressures, both of which were felt most keenly by Caputo himself as a combat officer: the pressure to produce bodies (the infamous "body count") as a way of measuring a unit's combat proficiency in the field—a tactic that resulted in the wholesale and indiscriminate killing of Vietnamese citizens; and the steady rate of attrition that Caputo's platoon suffered from booby traps and ambushes—a fact of warfare in Vietnam that quickly undermined Caputo's own sense of moral purpose. Eventually, he ordered the kidnapping of two Viet Cong suspects who were, in the event, "killed while trying to escape." The military investigation that followed was, to Caputo's mind, a farce designed not to apportion blame or even to reveal the truth, but merely to cover up the fact that "the war in general and US military policies in particular" were ultimately to blame for both American and Vietnamese deaths. To go on with the war, Caputo is forced to admit, was "worse than folly: it would be a crime, murder on a mass scale" (317). Caputo thus made a separate peace with himself and with the Viet Cong, and vowed never to fight again. "I was finished with governments and their abstract causes," he concludes, "and I would never again allow myself to fall under the charms and spells of a political witch doctor like John F. Kennedy" (315).

The investigation of what Caputo calls the "ambivalent reality" of the Vietnam experience appeared in one of its most intense forms with the publication in 1977 of Michael Herr's *Dispatches*—perhaps the most widely read, quoted, and praised book on the war. Herr was a journalist in Vietnam between 1967 and 1968, and like Greene and Halberstam before him, he was critically disposed to question the fundamental nature of America's presence in Vietnam. As with Kovic, Herr is bitter about the small-minded officialdom that got young "grunts" killed wholesale, and his insights into the mass-media myths that helped create the possibilities for Vietnam are equally to the point: "We'd all seen too many movies, stayed too long in Television Land, years of media glut had made certain connections difficult." Hence, Herr finds himself "thinking about all the kids who got wiped out by seventeen years of war movies before coming to Vietnam to get wiped out for good."[47]

Herr's book is an exploration of the connections between culture and experience, an attempt to explain not only what the war looked and felt like but also the meaning of his own ambivalent relationship to it. Whereas Greene and Halberstam chose to express their Vietnam experience in the form of the novel, Herr creates a highly subjective version of the personal journal. In generic terms, *Dispatches* represents an example of "new journalism." More specifically, *Dispatches* falls into a kind of journalistic phenomenology, where normative concepts of realism, disinterestedness, and objectivity are rejected in favor a personal immersion into the experience at hand. Traditional notions of authorial control are thus called into question in an exegesis that focuses on the contradictory and contingent nature of experience and reality. Meaning is not something that is simply assumed to exist in the world, independent of authorial consciousness and desire, but rather is constructed through language and interpretation.

Certainly, Herr makes no pretense of objectivity, attempting as he does to portray the multiple levels of his own often confused experiences as a participant-observer who often got too close to the violent actualities of the war. In this sense, *Dispatches* is as much a complex meditation on the perceptual density of the Vietnam experience as it is an investigation of the possibilities and difficulties of communicating that experience. What Herr discovers is that

> between the farout things you saw or heard and what you personally lost out of all that got blown away, the war made a place for you that was all yours. Finding it was like listening to esoteric music, you didn't hear it in any essential way through all the repetitions until your own breath had entered it and become another instrument, and by then it wasn't just music anymore, it was experience. (67)

But as Herr finds out, having gained the experience, he, like the rest of America, now has to learn to live with it: "You can't just blink it away," he writes, "or run the film backwards out of consciousness" (68).

Herr refuses to isolate the war as an event that can be explained in terms of faulty global strategies or the politics of inadvertence. The war in Vietnam had deep roots in American culture and history; nothing had happened over there, he writes, "that hadn't already existed here, coiled up and waiting" (268). Thus "you couldn't use standard methods to date the doom" in Vietnam because its origins and causes were essentially American. In this way, Herr's Vietnam is refigured as the return of a nightmarishly garbled frontier mythology, a "fatal environment" where "all the mythic tracks intersected, from the lowest John Wayne wet dream to the most aggravated soldier-poet fantasy" (19). For Herr, it "seemed the least of the war's contradictions that to lose your sense of American shame" it was necessary to get away from the "Mission" bureaucrats in Saigon, who "spoke goodworks and killed nobody themselves, and go out to the grungy men in the jungle who talked bloody murder and killed people all the time" (43–45). Out there in the bush was where certain "classic essential American types" found their true calling: "incipient saints and realized homicidals, unconscious lyric poets and mean dumb mother fuckers with their brains all down in their necks," the "redundant mutilators, heavy rapers, eye-shooters, widow-makers" (19). Here were the "point men, isolators and outriders," who seemed to be "programmed in their genes to do it, the first taste made them crazy for it, just like they knew it would" (35). At the other extreme were the Saigon "Dial Soapers" and "Mission flunkies," vicariously "bloodthirsting behind 10,000 desks," for whom Herr has little but contempt (43). As Herr makes clear, however, the greatest conceit of all is to consider yourself somehow separate from "the whole rotten mix" (31). You are, Herr insists, as responsible for what you see as you are for what you do, and Vietnam was the most intensely watched war in history.

Yet in spite of the miles of film and the hours of television, Herr contends that "something wasn't answered, it wasn't even asked." Hiding low under the "fact-figure crossfire there was a secret history, and not a lot of people felt like running in there to bring it out" (51). But it was there, "a hideous war and all kinds of victims," it was a "laughing death-face" hidden in every column of print and "held to your television screens for hours after the set was turned off for the night" (233). All the rest was "over-ripe bullshit . . . Hearts and Minds, Peoples of the Republic, tumbling dominoes, maintaining the equilibrium of the Dingdong by containing the ever encroaching Doodah" (19–20). The truth was uglier and more simple, Herr seems to be saying, and it can be summed up in the in the bitter cynicism of a young soldier: "We're here to kill gooks. Period" (20).

The real war was thus at base racist and unrelentingly murderous in its high-tech execution:

> A lot of people knew that the country could never be won, only destroyed, and they locked into that with breathtaking concentration, no quarter, laying down the seeds of the disease, roundeye fever, until it reached plague proportions, taking one from every family, a family from every hamlet, a hamlet from every province, until millions had died from it and millions more were left uncentered and lost in their flight from it. (62)

Although the soldiers in the field lived within this violent reality, the history was written somewhere else: "Nothing so horrible ever happened up-country that it was beyond language fix and press relations" (43). Thus the daily official briefing in Saigon become known as "the Five O'Clock Follies," or what Herr describes as an "Orwellian grope through the day's events as seen by the Mission" (105). It was a "psychotic vaudeville," writes Herr, but it was all dutifully quoted by the media who, therefore, gave legitimacy to it: "words that had no currency as words, sentences with no hope of meaning in the sane world" (229). The media got all the "facts," but

> it never found a way to report meaningfully about death, which of course was really what it was all about. Conventional journalism could no more reveal this war than conventional fire-power could win it, all it could do was take the most profound event of the American decade and turn it into a communications pudding, taking its most obvious, undeniable history and making it a secret history. (232)

Herr insists that two wars actually took place in Vietnam: the real war, in which people died in the hundreds of thousands, and a make-believe war that was the product of political expediency and public relations. The substance of Herr's book stems from his investigation of the contradictions that arise from that irreconcilable duality, where no one—neither author nor reader—can emerge disinterested or disengaged. Herr makes it clear that he is just as implicated in the war as those who fought it and those who, like him, watched and read about it.

Writing as one who had participated in the Vietnam War, Tim O'Brien addresses a different kind of duality in his novel *Going after Cacciato* (1978). O'Brien's protagonist, Paul Berlin, attempts to reshape the confusions and chaotic excesses of combat through an imagined flight from the war. That flight takes the form of a fantasy chase after a young soldier, Cacciato, who has fled the horrors of the war and is walking to Paris. Although the trek to Paris in search of Cacciato takes place only in Berlin's mind, it nevertheless represents an attempt to impose a personal order on the confusions of the war. In contrast to the endless and seemingly pointless patrols through the hostile Vietnamese countryside, the imagined chase across the continents to Paris has at least a discernable goal and a final destination. It is a movement toward an established and recognizable civilization, on the one hand, but also a return to the symbolic ground of World War II—a war that had knowable objectives. (Hence, the significance of the protagonist's name, Berlin, which marks both an objective and an endpoint of a previous war as well as the site of an ideological and political division.) What Berlin is in flight from, then, is the fateful terrain of America's war in Vietnam. Although Vietnam, too, is an older civilization, it is also alien and strange to the American troops, and its people are consequently unknowable:

Not knowing the language the men did not know whom to trust. Trust was lethal. They did not know false smiles from true smiles,

or if in Quang Ngai a smile had the same meaning it had in the
States. "Maybe the dinks got things mixed up," Eddie once said
after the time a friendly-looking farmer bowed and smiled and
pointed them into a minefield. . . . "Maybe when you smile over
here it means you're ready to cut the other guy's throat." . . . Not
knowing the people they did not know friend from enemies. They
did not know if it was a popular war, or, if popular, in what sense.
They did not know if the people of Quang Ngai viewed the war
stoically, as it sometimes seemed, or with grief, as it seemed other
times, or with bewilderment or greed or partisan fury. It was
impossible to know.[48]

In the same way, the environment of Vietnam, with its
jungles, paddies and seemingly primitive villages surrounded
by dense hedges, offered nothing familiar to which the soldiers might relate: "the hedgerows expressed the land's secret qualities: cut up, twisting, covert, chopped and mangled,
blind corners leading to dead ends, short horizons always
changing. It was only a feeling. A feeling of marching through
a maze, the feeling that mice must have as they run mazes. A
sense of entrapment mixed with mystery" (300).
The sense of mystery that the Vietnamese land and people inspire in the soldiers is intensified by the soldiers' ignorance of why they are in Vietnam and what the war is about:

He didn't know who was right, or what was right; he didn't
know if it was a war of self-determination or self-destruction, out-
right aggression or national liberation; he didn't know which
speeches to believe, which books, which politicians; he didn't
know if nations would topple like dominoes or stand separate like
trees; he didn't know who started the war, or why, or when, or
with what motives; he didn't know if it mattered. (313)

The Vietnam War, from the point of view of the foot soldier, was thus a formless affair with "no sense of order or
momentum" (320). It was, as Alfred Kazin puts it, "the ultimate no place to be"; it was a claustrophobia of such intense
proportions that the soldiers felt "imprisoned" and at the
mercy of "mysterious forces."[49] But more than this, as O'Brien
makes clear, the feeling that many soldiers had of being swept

up into the terror of Vietnam ultimately reflected back on the home culture. They had been sent to Vietnam for no discernable reason and abandoned there. A character in James Webb's *Fields of Fire* (1978) gives voice to that feeling: "We're prisoners here, We're prisoners of the war. . . . We been kicked off the edge of the goddamn cliff. They don't know how to fight it, and they don't know how to stop fighting it."[50] O'Brien calls it a war with no "substance. Aimless . . . a bunch of kids trying to pin the tail on the Asian donkey. But no fuckin tail. No fuckin donkey" (131).

By the time *Going after Cacciato* appeared in 1978, the Vietnam War debate was changing dramatically, as such popular films as *Coming Home, The Deer Hunter,* and *Apocalypse Now* began to affect the way people thought about the war. I discuss those films more fully in chapter 4; what I want to suggest here is that the novels and memoirs had established a complex sense of loss and ambivalence, much of which was extremely critical of American culture and politics. The film industry, of course, soon appropriated and reworked this written war, and by the beginning of the 1980s the war had reentered the living room by way of television, either as a subject or barely disguised subtext. According to one television critic, during the 1970s "Vietnam was like a plague. . . . If you touched it, your arm would rot away." By the 1980s, however, the TV networks began to "sidle up to the subject."[51] The Vietnam War was being partially reclaimed by the popular-culture industries as an authenticating experience for the heroes of such TV action-adventure series as *Magnum, P.I.* and *The A Team.* The Vietnam veteran was no longer the cultural outsider or social pariah, in TV drama at least, and the Vietnam experience was no longer the site of a male identity in crisis—not exclusively, at any rate. Indeed, the shifts surrounding the mass cultural marketing of Vietnam between 1978 and 1981 are paradigmatic of the wider ideological changes at work that announced the rise of new conservative forces in the United States.
    That this reforging of conservative influences in American

culture would involve an obsession with military spending and foreign policy was made clear early in Ronald Reagan's 1980 campaign for the presidency. The United States, he claimed, had "an inescapable duty to act as tutor and protector of the free World," but in order to carry out that God-ordained mission, "we must first rid ourselves of the Vietnam syndrome."[52] Now proclaimed a noble cause, the Vietnam War became the subject of intense political, cultural, and historical revisionism. The mystifying ideology of the quagmire would now become the most common approach to the Vietnam War—an approach that mystifies the war as a quirky anomaly and elides the human costs involved in a war that veterans such as Philip Caputo had witnessed as "murder on a mass scale."[53] In these circumstances, a new generation came of age knowing little about the Vietnam War except what could be gleaned from the various mass cultural rewritings that were, by the mid-1980s, an established staple of the movie and publishing industries. It is that particular aspect of growing up in the aftermath of Vietnam and the 1960s that forms the central theme of Bobbie Ann Mason's *In Country* (1985).

Mason's novel examines the war's impact on American culture as it has been registered on the post–baby boom generation, for whom the war is experienced as an absent presence that permeates contemporary culture yet remains mysterious and undefinable. As such, the war continues to construct political discourses and cultural identities, no longer as an immediate event that must be faced, but as a structuring absence that must first be rediscovered. What Mason's novel makes clear, however, is the near impossibility of reclaiming an "authentic" sense of the Vietnam War from either the historical writings of professional intellectuals or the variety of creative rearticulations offered by the culture industries.

Set in a small Kentucky town, Hopewell, in the summer of 1984, *In Country* depicts the struggles of Samantha (Sam) Hughes as she attempts to come to terms both with the historical legacy of Vietnam and her own personal investment in recovering the past. Her quest for authentic knowledge about Vietnam is motivated by a number of pressing concerns that have, as the novel opens, recently gained a sense of urgency following Sam's graduation from high school. Sam's father was killed in Vietnam before she was born, leaving her to be raised by her mother and her uncle Emmett, a Vietnam veteran, and then by her uncle alone after her mother remarries and moves to Lexington. The decentering effect of her family experience has produced in Sam a strong sense of her own independence, which is at the same time permeated by an ambivalence toward the cultural conventions of her social and sexual identity. Thus Sam is temporarily without direction in life; unable to move forward into the future of a college life away from home, and resisting the temptation to settle down in Hopewell, Sam is driven by an obsession with the Vietnam War and by the determination to find out what her father was really like.

Although Sam has read many of the "dull history books" that deal with the war and has seen all the films, the war and her father remain mysterious and obscure. Consequently, she is drawn to pester her uncle Emmett and other local veterans about their experiences in Vietnam. But as one of the veterans explains to her: "Sam, you might as well just stop asking questions about the war. Nobody gives a shit. They've got it twisted around in their heads what it was about, so they can live with it and not have to think about it."[54]

Sam also reads all the letters that her father sent from Vietnam and searches through his war diary for clues to his life. But in the end, she cannot get beyond her own experiences and into her father's, any more than she can imagine what it was like in Vietnam apart from the impressions of war she has absorbed from novels, television, and films. She tries to imagine the experience of jungle warfare in Vietnam, but eventually realizes that she "couldn't get hickory trees and maples and oaks . . . out of her mind" (210). In an attempt to recreate her father's Vietnam experience as her own, Sam camps out in a local swamp:

It hit her suddenly that this nature preserve in a protected corner of Kentucky wasn't like Vietnam at all. The night sky in Vietnam was a light show. . . . Rockets, parachute flares, tracer bullets, illumination rounds. . . . She tried to remember the descriptions she had read. It was like fireworks. And the soundtrack was different from bugs and frogs: the *whoosh-beat* of choppers, the scream of jets, the thunder-boom of artillery rounds, the mortar rounds, random bullets and bombs and explosions. The rock-and-roll sounds of war. (214)

Sam realizes that the soundtrack in her mind is actually "from *Apocalypse Now*—the Doors moaning ominously, 'This is the end . . . the children are insane'" (215). And so it goes whenever Sam tries to imagine what it had been like for her father. Even when her uncle Emmett, a veteran suffering from the effects of Agent Orange, tries to describe what Vietnam was like, she can only imagine the war in terms of scenes from the television series M*A*S*H.

The process of Sam's coming of age in the 1980s stands in a paradoxical relationship to the violent rite-of-passage scenarios in the novels and memoirs of Vietnam veterans. Undoubtedly, that relationship has everything to do with Sam's identity as a woman (her oedipal fixation and search for origins are not the same as those of the male veterans she interrogates), and to her status as secondhand observer—as witness to the post–Vietnam War era. For Sam's generation, Vietnam exists as a procession of simulations, a circuit of intertextuality that endlessly refers only back to itself. Sam's search for meaning and identity is ultimately trapped within that circuit of Vietnam revisionism, and in the end, all she can conjure up are her experiences of the war in popular culture. To be sure, authors such as Kovic and Caputo testify continually to their own sense of having been duped by the mythology of heroism promoted both by popular culture and political rhetoric. And, indeed, for most Americans, Vietnam had always been a simulated affair, a spectacle of the real: a television event, a grim report in the morning newspaper, a political abstraction that found perhaps its most dramatic representation in the street theater and riots of the 1960s. In the changed conditions of the 1980s, however, those who desired to recover, and to understand, the past were forced to confront the complexity of revisionism and the war's links to popular culture. Thus even those who might write the war—whether from the public archives or from personal experience—could not escape the need to explore, and to question, the conventions and limitations of its representation.

4

VIETNAM IN HOLLYWOOD

What finally distinguishes this latest effort from
earlier ones in the process involved here is the
tendency to take the loss of the war more seriously
than the war itself. What does it mean to win or
lose a war? . . . To win or lose a war reaches so
deeply . . . into the fabric of our existence that our
whole lives become that much richer or poorer in
symbols, images, and sources.

WALTER BENJAMIN, "THEORIES OF GERMAN FASCISM"

ONE OF THE problems of coming to terms with
the Vietnam War, as Sam Hughes discovers in *In Country*, is
that the war is no longer a specific cultural event, if indeed it
ever was—it does not "exist" out there somewhere, waiting
to be summoned up into representation. The war consists
instead of a dialectic between representational practices and
historical experience. It remains a contested terrain where
memory, ideology, and cultural processes intersect. Without
a doubt, much of the contemporary understanding of Vietnam, and of the intertextual and representational horizon
within which that understanding operates and is articulated,
owes a great deal to the mass circulation of cinematic recon-
structions of the war.

This is not to imply, however, that the Vietnam War has
been entirely "sanitized and Norman Rockwellized," to bor-

row from Paul Fussell's complaint against what he terms the "Disneyfied" representations of World War II. For unlike World War II, which "brought forth . . . the tuneful *South Pacific*," Vietnam was too closely and critically observed for the "tricks of publicity and advertising" to sweeten entirely the violent actualities of modern warfare in a small Third World country. According to Fussell, "television and a vigorous moral journalism," among other things, forced a "pap-fed mass audience" to face the "unpleasant facts" of America's war policy in Vietnam.[1]

While Fussell's observations offer an insightful and even compelling analysis of the differences between the cultural appropriations of the two wars, he fails ultimately to grasp the complex ways in which the Vietnam War has been rewritten and refigured in popular culture. While it is certainly true that "Disneyfied" musical celebrations of the war in Vietnam have yet to emerge, there is plenty of evidence to suggest that the subject of Vietnam can profitably be set to music. Although I return to this point later, it is perhaps necessary to point out here that in an age of MTV and video-packaged music, the Vietnam War has proved to be a usable musical package itself. And as a consequence, the tragedy and drama of the war has been rewritten in terms of melodrama—that quintessential form for exploring the tragic loss of culturally viable desires and identities.

Nevertheless, there have been more and less critical representations of the Vietnam War over the past two decades, and taken together, these have helped to establish a representational horizon within which a good deal of what is presently circulated under the sign of Vietnam is consumed. Although this particular distribution of signs and sounds operates in culture somewhat differently from the circulation of Vietnam literature, the two forms are, in the last instance, connected at the general level of cultural understanding. While the formal structures of cinematic narratives, along with the historical process through which popular audiences come to internalize the conventions of film narratives, constitute a semiautonomous practice, that practice is in no sense removed from the intellectual conflicts and political controversies or, indeed, from any of the historical and cultural problematics that are involved in the project of representing the lost war in Vietnam.

It is generally assumed, however, that Hollywood refused to face the unpleasant facts of American involvement in Vietnam while the war was taking place and that it subsequently neglected the subject in the years following. That current of opinion surfaced most vocally following the popular success of *Platoon* in 1986. *Platoon*, it was claimed, finally signaled Hollywood's rediscovery of its conscience. *Time* magazine, for example, greeted *Platoon* as a historically unique event: "Twenty years after it tore apart the nation's conscience, the Vietnam War reaches the screen with searing power and immediacy."[2] The implication here is that the American film industry had finally found it profitable to make a film about Vietnam. But a more general assumption underlying that view is one that David Halberstam articulated in his contemporary review of *Platoon*. Halberstam writes that, by its very nature, "the movie industry has been a notorious cheat when it comes to confronting serious subjects, and on Vietnam in particular there was a rare schizophrenic attitude on the part of the film industry's leaders."[3] In his view, the initial dearth of Vietnam War films is a specific example of the American film industry's pathological inability to confront controversial topics, topics that question, rather than confirm, established myths and ideologies. Hollywood declined to get involved in the Vietnam War, precisely because there appeared to be no way of approaching the subject without automatically alienating large numbers of potential viewers.[4]

That assessment of Hollywood is to a certain extent correct, and yet it is not the whole story. Throughout its history the American film industry has been quite successful in identifying ideological conflicts and social contradictions and resolving them symbolically within the conventions of popular film genres. That does not mean that Hollywood's approach to controversial topics involves direct or "realistic" portrayals of social problems. Rather, the usual Hollywood strategy is one that involves condensation and displacement—a strategy in which metaphorical and symbolic solutions are proposed within the conventions of established narrative genres. For instance, it has been persuasively argued that the popular Warner Brothers backstage musicals of the early 1930s, while typically characterized as fantasies created merely to distract the Depression-era audiences, were actually pro–New Deal proposals for an interclass cooperation and the subordination of excessive individualism to the common good in a time of intense economic and social dislocation.[5] Similarly, Westerns have been analyzed in terms of their articulation of contemporary social consciousness and their displacement of real social anxieties onto a mythic frontier landscape. The Western, in this view, is not in any simple sense about the history of the frontier; it is rather a narrative vehicle for working out contemporary anxieties generated, for example, during the Cold War, in which the struggle between West and East, self and other, could be satisfactorily, if temporarily, resolved within the Western genre.[6]

In that sense, all forms of cultural production emerge from, and can be viewed as, attempts to forward fictive resolutions to real political and social problems and contradictions. Fredric Jameson argues, for example, that movies do not merely reflect dominant ideology; instead, the very conventions that structure cinematic forms are themselves ideological in that they work to appropriate, set the limits, and propose fictional solutions to problems that are unresolvable within the context of everyday life. Although Jameson's argument might appear merely to rehearse a pessimistic and instrumentalist model of a totally "administered" and manipulated mass culture, he is, in fact, proposing something quite different. In contrast to the view that posits the popular-cultural audience as distracted, bemused, and ideologically interpolated into forms of "false consciousness," Jameson is concerned to uncover the procedures through which popular forms work to transform real social and political anxieties, fantasies, and desires into manageable narrative structures where they can be temporarily articulated, displaced, or resolved all together. As Jameson puts it:

> To rewrite the concept of a management of desire in social terms . . . allows us to think repression and wish fulfillment together within the unity of a single mechanism, which gives and takes alike in a kind of psychic compromise or horse-trading, which strategically arouses fantasy content within careful symbolic containment structures which defuse it, gratifying intolerable, unrealizable, properly imperishable desires only to the degree to which they can again be laid to rest.[7]

"Laying to rest" the intolerable and imperishable desires and fantasies generated by the Vietnam War within the strategic containment of a single mechanism describes, in a precise way, the ideological work performed by popular culture in general and by Vietnam War films in particular. As I have already mentioned, a good deal of this cultural work is aimed at deactivating the memory of both the war and, more crucially, the widespread political radicalism that the war both generated and intensified.

On another level, the same process of transformation and cultural "rehabilitation" works to (further) suppress the Vietnamese "enemy" as part of a restructuring of masculine subjectivity and identity in the aftermath of defeat. For example, beginning with *The Green Berets* (1968), continuing with *Go Tell the Spartans* and *The Boys in Company C*, and reaching an extreme in *The Deer Hunter* (all three films released in 1978), the Vietnamese "enemy" emerged as the psychic other—a menace and threat to the American myth of heroic masculinity. Symbolically, the Vietnamese guerrilla at once absorbs and organizes a range of anxieties, in particular "the haunting and unmentionable persistence of the organic—of birth, copulation and death"; those aspects of life normally suppressed or "sanitized by means of a whole strategy of linguistic euphemisms."[8] *Go Tell the Spartans*, for example, offers us three distinct Vietnamese groups: the South Vietnamese political leadership (corrupt and unreliable), friendly

Vietnamese (childlike, trusting, and ultimately left to their fate), and the Viet Cong (a deadly and faceless mass to be mown down by American firepower). In this film, none of the Vietnamese are shown to have any specific redeeming qualities (aside from a passive trust in American authority) and even the "friendlies," exemplified by the figure of the tellingly named Cowboy, display a casual brutality toward human life and a penchant for torture. Moreover, the problem of deciding precisely which Vietnamese are friendly and which are hostile is one of the organizing principles of the film. Indeed, it is a problem that recalls a well-established theme in popular historical representations, namely, the place of the American Indian in Hollywood Westerns.

Alan Trachtenberg has noted, for example, that the destruction and dispersion of the Indian nations, and the wholesale slaughter that often accompanied the imposition of the reservation policy, resulted in an Indian presence that has been displaced into a persistent "underside, the lasting bad conscience, within the prevailing conception of the 'West,' calling for repeated ritualistic slaying in popular Westerns."[9] Only bearable in the disguise of myth and ritual, this "secret script" of history reveals itself as the destructive horror that accompanied American expansion and development. When we also take into account the ideological function of myths and rituals, then, not surprisingly, the often bestial representations of the Vietnamese to be found in, for example, *The Deer Hunter*, or more persistently in *Rambo: First Blood II* and in the spate of "MIA" films that followed, functioned as convenient canon fodder for an American heroism in need of a cathartic redemption. Whereas the "winning" of the West generated a range of narratives and images that, until the late 1960s, celebrated the civilizing mission of white male heroes and accepted the stereotypes of the savage other, the American defeat in Vietnam has not been quite so easily displaced and suppressed.

In the case of the frontier period, Western movies turned to an established array of stereotypes, conventions, and narrative formulas: for example, the dime novels, the popular action prints of Frederic Remington, the various Wild West shows, popular histories and memoirs from the earliest captivity narratives to Theodore Roosevelt's *The Winning of the West* (1889–96). Frederick Jackson Turner's "frontier thesis" celebrated "the heroic masculine traits" of the pioneer and elevated the appropriation and exploitation of the West to the intellectual center of American historiography.

The Vietnam War, by contrast, presents a different set of problems and has called forth a different set of strategies. For one thing, the cultural certainties, stereotypes, and formulas that the Western had relied upon to project its version of heroic action were at least temporarily played out by the late 1960s. In the face of an intense generational debate over the meaning of heroism, and the ideological relationship between a tradition of valorized heroic activity and state power, the old verities of Western movie heroes no longer seemed viable. The conduct of the war, moreover, and the pervasive public perception of widespread atrocities and needless civilian deaths, could not be easily dismissed or put to rest. Hence, when film producers turned their attention to Vietnam in the 1970s, the old ideals of male authority and heroism had to be rethought. Vietnam, in other words, remained a live issue, even as the memory of the war receded into the past and was subjected to an often contentious process of revisionism. The clash of ideologies and counterideologies that made the Vietnam War a controversial and divisive domestic issues was thus "impressed on a culture as on a palimpsest, shaping and coloring all the images that evolve at later dates."[10]

Nevertheless, the very fascination with war and destruction, as Walter Benjamin argued in the 1930s, must be understood in relation to twentieth-century aesthetic forms that organize vision and perception in particular ways. Film and photography, for example, appear to bring us closer to experience through a visually mediated—and distanced—perspective. In film, war becomes a spectacle staged for the cinematic spectator, constructed as the all-perceiving eye. Aside from film, there are video games that simulate war from a variety of perspectives (the cockpit of a fighter plane, the sighting apparatus of a tank). Film and video footage taken by attack planes in combat have become the stock images of news broadcasts and documentaries. Such proliferation of war imagery has saturated the experience of a culture to the point where an aesthetic of contemplation and an aesthetic of destruction have become indistinguishable. That point was vividly demonstrated during the Persian Gulf War, when selected video footage of "smart bombs" blowing up bridges and buildings dominated "reporting" and were replayed on nightly television constantly.

In modern warfare, or in what Paul Virilio terms "industrialized warfare," the "representation of events" outstrips the "presentation of facts." According to Virilio, that emphasis has amounted to the supremacy of the image over the object to the point where we all now live within cultures dominated by the "logistics of military perception."[11] The history of this form of cultural perception runs parallel to, and is in fact entangled with, the history of the social and technological development of cinema. As Virilio explains, the development of repeating weapons and repeating images are part of the same historical process. More to the point, "the true war film" does "not necessarily have to depict war or any actual battle. For once the cinema was able to create surprise (technical, psychological, etc.), it effectively came under the category of weapons."[12]

This is not to suggest that a film projects a unitary meaning or a single ideological message. The process of encoding a mass cultural text is always an unstable process that cannot guarantee the ways in which various sections of the audience will decode it. Nevertheless, given the present-day fascination with Vietnam combat films, it is worth repeating Susan Sontag's warning concerning the social and psychological role that mass-produced fantasies play in modern societies. By their very repetition, films—even films critical of the Vietnam debacle—tend to "normalize what is psychologically unbearable, thereby inuring us to it."[13] We might also add that, through repetition, Vietnam representations inure us to unbearable ideological contradictions that, at some level, are their real subject.

From the 1960s to the present, various Vietnam War films have revealed just such a process of either grappling with or failing to address directly an ideological problematic that is unbearable in the raw. Symptomatic in this regard is *The Green Berets* (1968), a John Wayne vehicle dependent on the conventions and ideological forms of the Western genre and World War II movies. Although historians and critics are still undecided about the actual economic success or failure of *The Green Berets*, there is nevertheless some agreement concerning its failure as a war movie in general, and as a portrayal of the Vietnam War in particular—a point I will return to later in this chapter. But perhaps most tellingly, no one in Hollywood attempted to follow Wayne's example, and the film inspired no imitators. Indeed, it could be argued that Hollywood went in the opposite direction, in that public anxieties about the war invariably took the cinematic form of a concern about the return of potentially violent veterans to civilian life in the late 1960s and 1970s.

Whereas some post–World War II films, such as *The Best Years of Our Lives* (1946), had been willing to portray the returning veterans in terms of a range of class experiences (and as an often distraught cross-section of different and not necessarily positive war experiences), their final scenes were always concerned to stress the returning soldier's psychic recuperation and social integration. Vietnam veterans, by contrast, tended to be portrayed as beyond redemption; they were seen, in fact, as a positive threat to the social order. In this way, the symbolic landscape of the war, the terrain upon which the crucial battles of the war were decided, became America itself, and the immediate enemy and threat to society was now the estranged veteran.

In such early B movies as *Angels from Hell* (1968), *Satan's Sadists* (1969), *Chrome and Hot Leather* (1971), and *The Losers* (1971), Vietnam veterans were either equated with outlaw motorcycle gangs or set in violent opposition to them.[14] In

Elia Kazan's *The Visitors* (1972), two veterans who raped and murdered a Vietnamese woman return to wreak vengeance on the family of a buddy whose conscience had forced him to report the incident. This theme of bringing the war home with a vengeance was continued with *Welcome Home Soldier Boys* (1972), in which a group of returning veterans lay waste to a whole town following a series of petty insults. In one form or another, the potential for violence among returned veterans became a cultural obsession, finding expression in such films as *Magnum Force* (1973), *The Stonekiller* (1973), *Tracks* (1975) *The Enforcer* (1976), *Taxi Driver* (1976), *Heroes* (1977), and *Rolling Thunder* (1977). (Significantly, each of these films culminates in a violent confrontation and shootout.) To the dismay of many Vietnam veterans, the trend was transported wholesale to television, where throughout the 1970s veterans were characterized as dangerously unstable individuals.[15] In a decade-long series of moves that shifted perceptions of the Vietnam veteran from social pariah to cultural hero, this subgenre would reemerge in its most financially successful form with the release of *First Blood* in 1982. By that time, however, destruction would result not from group effort, an eruption of the collective experience of Vietnam, but from the technical skill and physical prowess of the singular Rambo.

The Western genre, as I have intimated, had for decades served as the most popular vehicle for mythic resolutions of conflict-ridden, ambiguous, and ideologically tangled issues.[16] By the opening of the 1970s, however, the Western formula had shifted and can be said to have broken down because it could no longer absorb the sheer intensity of emotions produced by the war abroad and the social conflicts at home. Consequently, the Western hero no longer functioned as the mediator between the forces of savagery and civilization, but was more likely to be portrayed as a self-interested entrepreneurial bounty hunter (Clint Eastwood in *For a Few Dollars More* [1967] or in *The Good, the Bad, and the Ugly* [1968]). Increasingly, the forces of law and civilization came to be represented in terms of a corrupt conspiracy of malevolent capitalists (*The Wild Bunch* [1969], *McCabe and Mrs. Miller* [1971], *Pat Garret and Billy the Kid* [1973]), and the traditional villains became heroes in such films as *Butch Cassidy and the Sundance Kid* (1969), *Bad Company* (1972), and *The Missouri Breaks* (1976). Moreover, the position of American Indians within the Western film also came in for a good deal of revisionism. In *Soldier Blue* (1970) and *Little Big Man* (1970) the massacre of entire Indian villages had obvious resonances for a public that had grown uneasy with the conduct of the Vietnam War, particularly after having witnessed burning Vietnamese villages on nightly television news broadcasts. And in *Chato's Land* (1972) and *Ulzana's Raid* (1972) the Indians became a symbolic Viet Cong, seeking revenge on a murderously arrogant frontier community.

The influence of the war was also felt on a number of other genres, especially as it affected attitudes toward authority and criticized the residual cultural and political values of an older generation. The sympathetic portrayal of the gangster couple in *Bonnie and Clyde* (1967), for example, found an enthusiastic audience among young Americans who seemed to identify with the anarchistic and nihilistic life-style of the cultural criminal—the outlaw, the alienated figure who no longer operated within the parameters of conventional social behavior. That authority triumphs in the end in no way invalidated Bonnie and Clyde's attempt to live by the light of their own countercultural romanticism. In fact, it validated it all the more because Bonnie and Clyde could be stopped only by an ambush that brought to bear an overwhelmingly one-sided firepower.[17] Significantly, the concept of the free-fire zone was not restricted to Vietnam, but was shown to have direct references in American history as well.

In many ways *The Graduate* (1967) and *Easy Rider* (1969) can be viewed as working within the same range of sentiments. Although neither film is concerned directly with the Vietnam War, both are nevertheless quintessential Vietnam-era films in that they give expression to the period's emergent anxieties—anxieties that the war would increasingly amplify and make more immediate. *The Graduate* locates youthful rebellion within an emerging awareness of the utter bankruptcy of middle-class values, which are shown to be crassly materialistic and sexually hypocritical. *Easy Rider* takes those themes several steps further in its portrayal of two counterculture figures who, on the proceeds of a lucrative drug deal, set out to ride their customized motorcycles across America. In the course of their travels it becomes increasingly apparent that American culture can be violently reactionary, especially toward those who reject conventional ways of signaling their sex: long hair, colorful dress, and a freewheeling style lead inevitably to violence and murder. Nevertheless, as with *Bonnie and Clyde*, films like *The Graduate* and *Easy Rider* are part of a wider cultural discourse that identified the tabooridden principles of the older generation—of "establishment" America—as sterile, violent, and oppressive. Conversely, the youthful and rebellious America of the counterculture was often portrayed in relation to an emergent idealism structured by the principles of honesty, spontaneity, and an unambiguous political sensibility.

Another film that responded to the 1960s antiwar sensibility was *Wild in the Streets* (1968), which traced the rise to national leadership of a rock 'n' roll star who, after achieving power, proceeds to banish everyone over thirty to prison camps where they are force-fed LSD. The basic message here was that the older generation was responsible for the problems of the world, including Vietnam, and therefore it was time for youth to take over the running of things.[18] The influence of campus revolts also found its way into the cinema with *The Strawberry Statement* and *Getting Straight* (both released in 1970), as did the politics, style, and music of the counterculture in such films as *Alice's Restaurant, Medium Cool, Zabriski Point,* and *Woodstock* (all released in 1969). Although the Vietnam War was often not represented directly in American films of the period, the conflicts that the war generated within the culture can be said to have had a powerful influence on film production in general.[19]

Significantly, the only Vietnam War combat film to appear at that time was *The Green Berets*, a film that was produced specifically as a challenge to Hollywood's abstract response to the war and as an overtly ideological statement in support of the war.[20] As such, it was from the start of its production a controversial intervention into a fractious cultural and political situation. Even though *The Green Berets* was a personal project of John Wayne's, and a project into which Wayne was willing to invest his not inconsiderable prestige and personal fortune, Hollywood was at best lukewarm toward the film, and many in the industry were openly hostile to its approach. Indeed, Universal, the studio that initially backed *The Green Berets*, broke its contract with Wayne rather than remain involved in what would obviously be a publicly contentious operation.[21]

President Johnson, on the other hand, was receptive to Wayne's personal request for government assistance in making *The Green Berets*. In a letter to Johnson, Wayne wrote that it was "extremely important that not only the people of the United States but those all over the world should know why it is necessary for us to be there [Vietnam]," and that "the most effective way to accomplish this is through the motion picture medium." The aim of the film, Wayne argued, was to "inspire a patriotic attitude on the part of fellow Americans."[22] Whatever his stated intentions, Wayne nevertheless needed to inspire the cooperation of the Department of Defense; in particular, he needed to persuade the department to lend its technical expertise and military equipment. In response to Wayne's inquiry, Johnson's personal aide Jack Valente advised that although Wayne's conservative politics ran counter to the administration's, his views on the Vietnam War were very much in line with the government's. And in one of those rare moments that not only reveal the general cynicism of political life but also bring to the fore the deep contradictions of the Johnson administration, Valente's memo to the president states: "If he [Wayne] made the picture he would be saying the things we want said."[23] Consequently, *The Green Berets* was given all the military assistance it needed, including helicopter gunships and other state-of-the-art weaponry, along with advisors, army extras, and the run of the army training facility at Fort Benning, Georgia.[24]

Despite such lavish military support (or perhaps because of it?), *The Green Berets* turned out to be a formulaic recycling of hackneyed themes and conventions that the popular films of the period had for the most part undermined. *The Green Berets* was thus received as a conventional action movie that drew on the residual collateral of John Wayne's movie persona; it was not, in other words, considered to be an "authentic" picture of the Vietnam War. Although the film was concerned with the various adventures of a Special Forces unit in Vietnam, it was also, as its producer, Michael Wayne, admitted, basically a "cowboys and Indian film" in which the "Americans are the good guys and the Viet Cong are the bad guys. It's as simple as that . . . when you are making a picture, the Indians are the bad guys."[25] In many ways, *The Green Berets* can even be read as a botched attempt to recreate the Western cavalry films in which Wayne starred under the direction of John Ford in the late 1940s. Leonard Quart and Albert Auster make this observation in their study of the Vietnam War film, and explain that "Wayne's Green Berets were a fortress of muscular and professional anti-communist values" in the same way that "Ford's cavalry units, perched at the edge of the frontier, were bastions of communal honor, tradition, camaraderie and pride, fighting an often little appreciated and less understood battle for civilization and decency against the barbarians."[26]

The important point, however, is that a vast cultural divide had opened up between the ideology of the 1940s and that of the late 1960s. Although John Ford's films might well have been viewed with a sense of nostalgia for a movie world long past (as they often are today), they no longer supplied relevant guidelines for the moviegoing public at the time of the Vietnam War. Moreover, the year in which *The Green Berets* was released—1968—was not a fortuitous one for overtly patriotic gestures in the direction of a moribund foreign policy. This was the year of the Tet Offensive in Vietnam, when all talk of a "light at the end of the tunnel" suddenly looked insanely optimistic, even to the most conservative sections of the public and the media. This was also the year of the My Lai massacre, an incident that quickly established itself as a symbol of the war's out-of-control barbarism. At home, there were the riots in Chicago, the march on the Pentagon, and the assassinations of Bobby Kennedy and Martin Luther King—the murder of King sparking yet additional riots in dozens of American cities and setting even deeper the frustrations of African-American troops in Vietnam. Even in the best of times, *The Green Berets* would have received an ambivalent critical response. In 1968 it was almost guaranteed a harshly critical reception.

It was, moreover, the film's overt ideological stance that provoked the wrath of the critics. Even the Hollywood trade papers, which are generally somewhat subdued in their criticisms of the industry's products, were unusually harsh in their reaction to *The Green Berets*. It is a "cliché-ridden throwback" to World War II "potboilers," wrote the critic for the *Hollywood Reporter*, "its artifice readily exposed by the nightly actuality of TV news coverage." Furthermore, as this critic continues, the film's "facile simplifications" were "unlikely to attract the potentially large and youthful audience whose concern and sophistication cannot be satisfied by the insertion of a few snatches of polemic."[27] Indeed, it would be almost a decade before Hollywood was once again to treat the subject of combat in Vietnam in anything approaching a serious manner—and in anything approaching a sustained effort to garner a potentially large and youthful audience. This is not to say that war itself ceased to be a popular and even a profitable movie topic. Fairly popular films such as *Patton* (1970) and *Tora, Tora, Tora* (1970) openly flaunted their sense of nostalgia for the seemingly moral clarity of World War II—or what Studs Terkel has called the "Good War." Even here, however, the retelling of World War II had to coexist with the satire and black humor of *Catch 22* (1970) and *M*A*S*H* (1970), both of which addressed the sense of ambivalence and alienation that the Vietnam War had created among the sixties generation. But when Hollywood eventually got around to making films about Vietnam, there would be few resemblances to either World War II movies or *The Green Berets.*

APOCALYPTIC VISIONS AND HOLLYWOOD CONVENTIONS

As the passion and moral fervor over the Vietnam War began to subside in the post-Watergate era of the late 1970s, there began to develop within American culture a curiosity—and eventually an underlying guilt—about the experience the veterans had gone through in Vietnam. In large part, such widely read memoirs as Philip Caputo's *A Rumor of War,* Ron Kovic's *Born on the Fourth of July,* and most particularly, Michael Herr's *Dispatches* helped to stimulate that curiosity.

There also emerged a curiosity over what had happened to America in the Vietnam War era. As Morris Dickstein explains, Vietnam remained the major piece of "unfinished business" from the sixties: "In Vietnam we lost not only a war and a subcontinent; we also lost our pervasive confidence that American arms and American aims were linked somehow to justice and morality, not merely to the quest for power. America was defeated militarily, but the 'idea' of America, the cherished myth of America, received an even more shattering blow."[28]

Many historians tend to agree with Dickstein, particularly when they characterize the Vietnam War era as a time when America "came apart" or as a period that left a "wounded generation" in its wake. Metaphors of unhealed wounds, shattered myths, and ruined childhoods are to be found everywhere in the writings about the war and the 1960s, and they suggest the unfinished process of coming to terms with the empty spaces in both consciousness and language left by the defeat in Vietnam.[29] Any attempt to produce critically successful and popular films about the war in Vietnam would thus have to address this cultural landscape of loss and conflict. Not surprisingly, then, when Hollywood eventually turned fully toward the Vietnam War in the late 1970s, the three major box office successes, *Coming Home* (1978),

The Deer Hunter (1978), and *Apocalypse Now* (1979), did just that.

Of those three films, *Coming Home* is arguably the more overtly political in that its anti–Vietnam War message is immediately obvious and accessible (although one might ponder the usefulness of such a message more than a decade after U.S. troop numbers in Vietnam had reached their peak and three years after the last soldiers had left Saigon). The making of *Coming Home* was influenced by the experiences of Ron Kovic, whose story was known to both Tom Hayden and Jane Fonda.[30] Kovic's book, *Born on the Fourth of July*, would eventually be adapted for the screen by Oliver Stone. In fact, during the period of *Coming Home*'s production and release, Kovic and Stone were struggling to get their far grittier version of *Born on the Fourth of July* into production. Just four days before principle shooting was to begin, however, the film was canceled, and Kovic's story would have to wait until Stone's own story had been already successfully translated into the box office hit *Platoon*.

Unlike Kovic's sustained study in disillusionment, despair, and eventual awakening to collective political activism, set within the broader context of the war's social implications, *Coming Home* works within the conventional melodramatic framework of the love triangle. In the tradition of Hollywood's established approach to controversial topics, the consequences and liabilities of a discredited system of foreign policy and a politically corrupting war are displaced onto personal narratives that explore individual subjectivity. And as with many early attempts to represent Vietnam, the tendency is to aestheticize violence and displace political conflict onto romantic fictions of war.

The opening scene in *Coming Home*, for example, suggests that what is to follow will be a cinema verité documentary concerned with the plight of wounded Vietnam veterans. (In fact, the scene was shot at the Veterans Administration hospital in Downey, California, and features wounded Vietnam veterans.) In the first images of the film, a group of disabled veterans cluster around a pool table and "rap" about the war.

As they talk, the camera pans around the group, and their voices can be heard on the soundtrack debating whether they had done the right thing by fighting in Vietnam. In the meantime, the camera has focused on one section of the group and then slowly zooms in on the figure of Luke Martin (Jon Voight), who thus becomes the increasingly privileged figure within the frame. Luke is lying on a hospital gurney, seemingly deep in thought, while a veteran speaking off-camera ponders the significance of his experience: "I have to justify being paralyzed. I have to justify killing people, so I say Nam was O.K. But how many guys can say, 'What I did was wrong, man,' and still be able to live with themselves, 'cause they're crippled for the rest of their life?"

Even though we recognize Jon Voight in the final shot, all of the stylistic elements in this opening sequence—the grainy film stock, the natural lighting, the overlapping dialogue, the use of nonprofessional actors—contrive to establish a sense of cinematic and social realism. By privileging the character of Luke Martin within the veteran group, the camera provides us with the first clue to a narrative movement that will shift from the politics of the social collective to the emotional evolution of the individual. And from that point on, the emotional weight of the film will be carried by professional actors. Furthermore, the anger and self-doubt expressed through the dialogue of the veterans in the opening scene serve to map out the characteristics of Luke's future development as he is forced to come to terms with his Vietnam experience and his physical paralysis. Eventually, it will be Luke who admits that the Vietnam War is wrong, and who refuses to justify either the death and destruction of the war or the fact of his paralysis.

Using these spontaneous expressions of the Vietnam experience, *Coming Home* establishes its Hollywood credentials at the same time that it questions the conventional formulas upon which those credentials rest. In the end, however, the conventions win out, and *Coming Home* fairly quickly develops along the familiar lines of Hollywood melodrama. In this sense, the film prefigures what would become in the late

1980s a major structuring process in the rewriting of the Vietnam War, namely, war as a melodrama of interpersonal strife and emotional excess taking place within the American family, a theme I return to in chapter 5.

In contrast to *Coming Home*, *The Deer Hunter* presents the spectator with "the tragic grandeur of a popular epic" both in its scope and in its organization.[31] Like such Hollywood epics as *Gone with the Wind*, it attempts to recreate an entire world of experience. In fact, *Gone with the Wind* offers an apt comparison to *The Deer Hunter* because it, too, portrays a community of established values and rituals that are violently wrenched apart by internal contradictions and external threats. Even though the Pennsylvania steeltown setting of *The Deer Hunter* is a far cry from the embattled plantation culture of the South in the 1860s, *The Deer Hunter* nonetheless constructs a similarly nostalgic portrait of a community oddly isolated from the powerful political and cultural currents of wartime. It is a place wholly unto itself, structured in the social relations and rhythms of steel production and by the residual values of its Russian immigrant population. The tragedy of the community and its experience of the war stems from the tightly drawn network of an established working-class "structure of feeling" (to borrow Raymond Williams's term). This psychic and social milieu forms a grid of expectations in which war and combat are both valorized and invested with the tropes of masculine desire and identity.

The protagonists of *The Deer Hunter* are three young steelworkers: Michael (Robert De Niro), Nick (Christopher Walken), and Steven (John Savage). As the film opens, three important events are imminent: Steven is about to get married, Michael and Nick are planning to go hunting with friends immediately after the wedding, and all three men are leaving home to fight in Vietnam. This latter prospect is not projected as particularly unsettling, and the three seemingly politically innocent young men show few signs of hesitation or regret. It is left to Nick to articulate precombat anxieties; he makes Michael swear that no matter what happens in

Vietnam he is to make sure that Nick is not left behind. This quietly constructed scene not only suggests the special bond between Michael and Nick but also prefigures Michael's obsessive desire in the second half of *The Deer Hunter* to reconstitute the male group in the aftermath of Vietnam.[32]

Although Michael is the charismatic leader of the group, he is also something of an enigma to his friends. At various times in the film his friends refer to him as "crazy," as a "faggot," and as the "last virgin." On the other hand, as much as he is the binding force of the group, he is also shown to be disdainfully aware of his friends' shortcomings and is, on occasion, openly contemptuous of their childish pranks and lack of self-control. Michael also lives with Nick in a dilapidated house at the edge of town—between industry and nature. It is in nature, during the group's hunting trips to the mountains, that Michael seems most fully himself. In distinct contrast to the antics of his friends, Michael practices his credo of the "one shot"—the ideal of one clean shot to kill a deer. Whereas his friends are more of a danger to themselves on the hunt than they are to the deer, Michael is shown to be a patient and skillful hunter who relentlessly pursues the game until he is in a position to put his "one shot" credo into practice. That the spectator is meant to view the hunt as the apotheosis of Michael's character is made strikingly apparent by low-angle camera shots, which frame Michael against the purity of the clear sky and the clean sweep of the mountain peaks. At the same time a heavenly choir on the soundtrack elevates the scene to the level of a mythic purification ritual, thereby resonating with the tropes of Nazi filmmaking in 1930s Germany.

Michael is not glorified, however, as a supernaturally endowed *Übermensch* (the Rambo films of the 1980s would supply that element), yet he does fall within what Susan Sontag describes as the dominant preoccupations of a fascist aesthetic: a "longing for high places, of the challenge and ordeal of the elemental, the primitive . . . in which triumph over everyday reality is achieved by ecstatic self-control and submission." Sontag further explains how fascist texts are obsessed "with situations of control, submissive behavior, extravagant effort, and the endurance of pain"—a list of psychological and personality traits that accurately describes both Michael and the all-male group of which he is a member.[33] Finally, the film's title, *The Deer Hunter*, can also be interpreted as having a literary source more specifically American, namely, James Fenimore Cooper's *The Deerslayer*. Like Cooper's Natty Bumppo, Michael is a chaste loner caught between contending cultural traditions (individual and community, immigrant religious rituals and secular rationalism, country and city) and forced by historical circumstances to adapt his individual hunting skills to the collective demands of war. From the hyperdisciplined desire to take down a deer with a single shot to the mass killing of humans in modern warfare, Michael's skills are appropriated and warped in the killing fields of Vietnam.[34]

The Deer Hunter is divided into three broad narrative segments: before, during, and after the protagonists' tour of duty. The first segment involves a detailed portrait of the steel town community—Clairton, population 36,500—from the ending of the night shift, through the elaborate portrayal of Steven's Russian Orthodox wedding and reception, to the deer hunt that follows. The second and most controversial segment is situated in Vietnam, where Michael, Nick, and Steven are captured by the Viet Cong and forced to play Russian roulette. It is this scene that caused the most anger among the film's many critics who, quite rightly, protested the brutal racist stereotyping of the Vietnamese. In any event, the Russian roulette experience totally undermines Nick's psychological health, and during the escape, engineered by Michael, Steven is maimed when he falls from a rescue helicopter; he subsequently seeks to cut himself off from his former Clairton attachments. Only Michael survives the ordeal sufficiently intact to be able to return to Clairton, where, it is clear, nothing can ever be the same again. In the final section of the film, set shortly before the fall of Saigon, Michael returns to Vietnam in search of Nick, who has been AWOL since his release from a military hospital. He eventually finds a barely recognizable Nick, who is now addicted both to Russian roulette and to heroin—a one-shot credo of a different kind. In spite of Michael's best efforts to stop him (efforts that include an impassioned declaration of love), Nick participates in a Russian roulette game and is killed.

The three basic narrative segments are welded together by *The Deer Hunter's* metaphorical structure, a repeated sequence of images and motifs that gather increasing intensity as their thematic importance is developed. The first segment opens in fire—the relatively controlled fire of the steel mill where the three protagonists work. The second segment begins with the fire of war—explosions, napalm strikes, and the flamethrower used by Michael to kill an enemy. The fire is beginning to burn out of control, as the following scenes of capture and torture make clear. In the final segment, a whole world is going up in flames as Michael searches for Nick in the burning ruins of Saigon. Here the Promethean experience of the American mission in Vietnam is graphically portrayed and then underlined by Michael's failed attempt to rescue the burned-out Nick. A similar process of increasing metaphorical intensity also emerges from Michael's one-shot credo—a motif that erupts with murderous irony in the Russian roulette scenes. Those scenes also connect to a gambling motif that is established in the first narrative segment. Michael and Nick continually bet on everything from pool shots to hunting, and Nick always loses—just as he will ultimately lose the final Russian roulette gamble. In this way, motifs from the opening scenes are developed into dark metaphors that underline an evolving sense of the vulnerability and powerlessness of the three protagonists.

The film ends on a grim note as the remaining friends, including Steven in a wheelchair, bury Nick in Clairton and sing a sad rendition of "God Bless America." There is no sense of an affirmation in their singing; it is a mournful dirge that signifies the incomprehension underlying their sorrow. The Vietnam War has been a degenerative experience that has devastated the once-confident and boisterous male group.

Indeed, as the film critic Robin Wood writes, the narrative progress of *The Deer Hunter* begins in plenitude and ends in impoverishment; it begins with a wedding and ends with a wake.[35] Moreover, this principle of "dwindling" is enacted in the three protagonists: Nick is dead, Steven is a paraplegic, and Michael has lost his sense of authority and leadership. Male identity in *The Deer Hunter*, therefore, with its rituals of drinking and hunting, has not only been shaken but has also been fundamentally impaired by the Vietnam experience.

For all its epic qualities, however, *The Deer Hunter* was no more successful than *Coming Home* in revealing the political realities of the Vietnam War. It was, however, symptomatic of a psychic and emotional reality—a reality that spoke to many spectators of the intensity and disruptions of the Vietnam War era. In this, *The Deer Hunter* is similar to *Apocalypse Now*, only the latter film takes the premise of failed male identity to its surrealist extreme. Highly stylized and visually powerful, *Apocalypse Now* portrays the Vietnam War as an absurdist epic where helicopter squadrons blare out Richard Wagner's "Ride of the Valkyries" as they fly into battle, and where a whole village is destroyed for nothing more serious than to gain access to Vietnam's best surfing waves. Francis Ford Coppola's film, in short, is nothing less than a cinematic *Gesamtkunstwerk*, a work of art in which all the elements work together to a single purpose—simultaneously to criticize and aestheticize the distinctly American form of madness that lay at the heart of the war.

Apocalypse Now is loosely based on Joseph Conrad's short story "Heart of Darkness." Like Conrad's character Marlow, Coppola's protagonist Willard (Martin Sheen), a CIA hit man, is given a mission that will take him upriver and into the dark heart of the human capacity for violence and cruelty. More to the point, the mission will move inexorably through a series of spectacles, each becoming progressively more alienated and insane, until the journey takes Willard deep into the darkest cultural recesses of megalomaniacal brutality. As the journey proceeds, however, it becomes increas-

ingly clear that the American presence in Vietnam, even
when no specific harm is intended, is automatically destructive. The wake of the PT boat that carries Willard upriver, for
example, creates havoc for the river-dwelling Vietnamese,
tipping over their frail canoes and drenching all who are not
nimble enough to scramble up the riverbank.

Conrad's story supplies the outlines of the film's subjective, psychological journey, while the setting of the Vietnam
War gives that journey its external focus. The implications of
the mission to "terminate with extreme prejudice" (a CIA
euphemism for "assassinate") Colonel Kurtz (Marlon Brando)
is conveyed through Willard's subjective voiceover, through
which we learn Kurtz's history and the case for his execution.
Although once a trusted career officer, Kurtz has been driven
over the edge by the war and has set himself up as a warrior
god among the primitive people of the far jungle reaches. In
open rebellion against the way the American military is running the war, he has set out with his own private army to
exterminate the enemy with greater efficiency and thor-
oughness. Unhampered by ethical questions and military
bureaucracy, Kurtz wages a war that recognizes no borders or
laws and that counts all who stand in the way, including
Americans, as the enemy. "We must kill them all," Kurtz
raves, revealing the Nazi-style will to power at the heart of
his program: "We must incinerate them, pig after pig, cow
after cow, village after village, army after army. . . . Exterminate them all."

By the time Willard and Kurtz finally confront each other,
they have reached similar conclusions concerning the American conduct of the war: Willard thinks of his superior officers
as "a bunch of four-star clowns who are giving the whole cir-
cus away," while Kurtz views Willard as an "errand boy for
grocery clerks come to collect their price." Moreover, Willard
has witnessed the insanity and waste of the Vietnam War
for years and wonders what the commanding generals have
against Kurtz: "Charging someone with murder in this place
is like handing out speeding tickets at the Indianapolis 500."
Kurtz, too, poses a similar question: "What do you call it

when the assassins accuse the assassin?" Clearly, then, both Willard and Kurtz are products of the same kind of madness. While Kurtz has taken the logic of the war to its furthest extreme, rejecting the euphemisms and pseudomorality of the high command, Willard sympathizes with him. And although Willard does assassinate Kurtz in the end, his reasons for doing so are left murky and unstated. It is also unclear what Willard intends to do or where he intends to go once Kurtz is dead.

As in *Coming Home* and *The Deer Hunter*, there is no unambiguous resolution at the end of *Apocalypse Now.* We are left instead with a vision of alienation within the experience of Vietnam as Willard drifts downriver, away from the site of sacrificial assassination and back to the "official" war. Has Willard embraced the "eloquent phantom" of war's evil, or has he stepped back from that "threshold of the invisible," like Conrad's Marlow before him?[36] It is almost impossible to view the closing scene without invoking Conrad, but to do so only calls forth the ideological mystifications of an earlier epoch—the equivocations and ambivalence of Western imperialism as it was beginning to turn in upon itself in the early part of the twentieth century. In this sense Conrad's words, like Graham Greene's, reach across history in the form of tragedy that turns, almost inexorably, to farce. The following lines from "Heart of Darkness" might have been written by any number of Vietnam veteran writers, including Michael Herr, who wrote the dialogue for *Apocalypse Now*:

> I have wrestled with death. . . . It takes place in an impalpable greyness, with nothing underfoot, with nothing around, without spectators, without clamor, without glory, without the great desire of victory, without the great fear of defeat, in a sickly atmosphere of tepid skepticism, without much belief in your own right, and still less in that of your adversary. (100–101)

The inconclusive ending of *Apocalypse Now* leads us back to Conrad's musings on the fate of Western subjectivity, which attempts to control the primitive urges it encounters in the dark reaches of war and imperialistic arrogance. It also takes us forward to the American dilemma of finding meaning in the travesty of a mission that destroys what it had pledged to save. It is Kurtz's personal tragedy to discover that everything he believed in, and everything he thought he was achieving, is in fact hollow and meaningless. At least Conrad could claim the presence of an idealism (an idea) behind the imperialist drive toward ever more efficient and ideologically rationalized forms of exploitation of African lands and peoples. More importantly, for Conrad the idea was not "a sentimental pretence" but an "unselfish belief . . . something you can set up, and bow before, and offer a sacrifice to" (100). Unlike previous empires, whose "administration was merely a squeeze" enforced by violent suppression, Conrad viewed the British empire in Africa as representing an ideal worthy of devotion and sacrifice. In *Apocalypse Now* it is precisely the lack of any such enabling idealism behind the American war in Vietnam that finally undermines both Willard and Kurtz. The American frontier myth of bringing the light of civilization to the savage darkness of the wilderness is, in the figure of Kurtz, finally displayed as a self-interested "squeeze" upheld through "brute force." But even here Conrad's words are illuminating; for Conrad, too, realized that the experiences of those who become directly engaged in the struggle for empire are not necessarily free of ambiguity and guilt. "The best you can hope from it," he wrote, "is some knowledge of yourself—that comes too late—a crop of unextinguishable regrets" (100). As with Marlow, so with Willard and, by extension, so with America.

Following the release of *Apocalypse Now* in 1979, Hollywood's interest in the Vietnam War temporarily faded. Still, the films of the 1970s had established the Vietnam War as a topic replete with cinematic and ideological possibilities— and a topic that seemed to promise box-office profits. Overall, the cycle of 1970s Vietnam War films was constructed within the negative assumptions that marked the legacy of Vietnam in post-Watergate America. Perhaps more to the point, those films are examples of what Robin Wood calls the "incoherent" film texts of the 1970s. Wood argues that the questioning of authority spurred by Vietnam and Watergate lead inevitably to the "questioning of the entire social structure" that validates such authority. And yet that ideological crisis lead not to revolution but merely to congressional tinkering with the power of the executive branch. The social order seemed to be on the brink of disintegration, yet as Woods notes, "there was no serious possibility of the emergence of a coherent and comprehensive alternative."[37] It is this impasse that underlies the most important films of the 1970s, accounting not only for their ideological complexity but also for their nihilism.

The incoherence of film texts in the 1970s highlights their inability to contain or resolve the issues they raise. Wood examines *Taxi Driver* (1976), *Looking for Mr. Goodbar* (1977), and *Cruising* (1980) in an effort to demonstrate "that the issues and conflicts they dramatize can no longer even appear to be resolvable within the system, within dominant ideology."[38] This, I would claim, is precisely the case with the Vietnam War films of those years, particularly in terms of their problematic endings. In film after film, the final scenes open up multiple alternatives and readings, and thus refuse to provide a coherent or conclusive resolution.

Moving into the 1980s, the cultural landscape shifted once again, now into the age of Reaganism, which signaled the emergence of a conservative bloc of interests and programs that came to dominate the national agenda to the point where all currents of thought and practice were affected. Certainly, television programmers and film producers quickly adjusted to what they perceived as the "new mood" of the country. The "word was out in Hollywood," writes Todd Gitlin, "that the networks were buying fewer TV series and movies charged with potential controversy." More specifically, Gitlin notes, producers, writers, and performers were being told to stay away from "politically sensitive material."[39] President Reagan himself sent shudders through the industry when he began expressing concern over the "immoral" content of contemporary films. He even went so far as to advocate a return to the kind of rigorously imposed censorship that had existed in the days of the Hays Office and the Motion Picture Production Code. According to *Variety,* Reagan's statements caused "apprehension" and "alarm" throughout the film industry.[40] A particularly chilling sign of Reagan's continuing interest in the filmmaking world emerged with his appointment of Roy Brewer to the U.S. Advisory Council on Employee Welfare in late 1981. Brewer, like Reagan, had been a central figure in Hollywood's institutionalized system of blacklisting during the 1950s.[41]

In the spring of 1982 this so-called new mood found material expression when CBS canceled *Lou Grant,* one of the few television shows that had been willing to address such allegedly sensitive issues as, for example, nuclear holocaust, pollution, unemployment, and the plight of Vietnam veterans. Although everyone in the media business was aware of the political pressure that a number of conservative groups, including Jerry Falwell's Moral Majority, had exerted on network executives to cancel *Lou Grant,* the executives insisted on the fiction that the show was dropped because of poor ratings. Moreover, and aside from the question of the progressive leanings of *Lou Grant* as a prime-time television series, conservatives were particularly alarmed by Ed Asner, the show's politically outspoken leading star.[42]

Not only was Asner associated with a number of left-wing causes at the time of the show's cancellation (including residual elements of the sixties peace movement), but under his leadership the Screen Actors Guild had once again become an active political force in Hollywood. The immediate cause of Asner's problems, however, stemmed from his public support of the leftist rebels in El Salvador and his likening of U.S. activities in Central America to the Vietnam War. In response to Asner's activities, boycotts were organized against those companies that advertised their products on *Lou Grant.* Furthermore, President Reagan expressed himself publicly as being "very disturbed" by Asner's political leanings and the Screen Actors Guild's "drift into politics" under Asner's leadership.[43] Given those conditions, CBS moved quickly to distance itself from the increasingly controversial actor and his show.

Thus new cultural and political forces and new coalitions of power and influence began to make themselves felt in the early 1980s. In the films that opened the decade, two broad themes predominate: an inward focus on personal and domestic life, which marked such films as *Kramer vs. Kramer* (1979), *Ordinary People* (1980), and *On Golden Pond* (1981), and an outward focus on cartoonlike action, evident in such adventure and science fiction fantasy narratives as *The Empire Strikes Back* (1980), *Raiders of the Lost Ark* (1981), *Star Trek I* (1979), *Star Trek II* (1982), and *E.T.* (1982). Running parallel to those films was another trend, which one media scholar has termed "the rehabilitation of the U.S. military."[44] In stark contrast to the Vietnam films of the late 1970s, one finds a more positive portrayal of the military, and especially of the officer class, in such films as *Taps* (1981), *An Officer and a Gentleman* (1982), and *The Lords of Discipline* (1983). The trend continued with celebrations of the air force's "right stuff" in *Iron Eagle* (1986) and *Top Gun* (1986). By the mid-1980s there also appeared a series of films that reinstated the fear of Communist takeover, a theme that had not been seriously or overtly considered in the American cinema since the 1950s. In *Red Dawn* (1985), *Invasion U.S.A* (1985), and the television miniseries *Amerika* (1987), the possibility of a Soviet takeover is predicated on the notion that the Vietnam syndrome has sapped the American people's will to resist. That such films were attempting to give cinematic expression to the rhetoric of the New Right is evidenced in the presence of Nicaraguan Sandinista troops in the various invasion scenarios—a representational fallout from the new domino theory that had come to fashion Latin American foreign policy along lines that resembled the discredited Vietnam policy.

It was within this network of intertextuality that a new cycle of Vietnam War films emerged. Of the diverse protagonists of those films, the only one to enter the Pantheon of American cultural icons was Rambo. Johnny Rambo represents the profound sense of disillusionment generated by the loss of the war in Vietnam (especially among those conservative groups who insisted that America was stabbed in the back by home-front doves), and the subsequent need for at least symbolic reassurances that the blame could be placed somewhere within the liberal-corporate state. In *First Blood* (1982), Rambo's anger is initially directed against a complacent citizenry who care nothing for the sacrifices he has made for his country as a Green Beret in Vietnam. The conflict begins when the sheriff of a small Northwestern town attempts to move Rambo (Sylvester Stallone) on, believing him to be a vagrant and potential troublemaker. When Rambo refuses to be hustled out of town, he is arrested and thrown into jail, where unsympathetic police officers try forcibly to clean him up and cut his hair. The result is that Rambo—in the midst of a flashback to scenes of torture while a prisoner of the North Vietnamese—lashes out with all the deadly skill of his Special Forces training. Escaping from the jail and into the nearby mountain forest, Rambo sets out on a one-man guerrilla war against the sheriff's posse and, subsequently, the National Guard. In effect, he becomes the Viet Cong, seemingly at home in the forest and, in words that in many ways announced Hollywood's new generation of Vietnam films, able to bring home to his enemies "a war you'll never believe."

Eventually, having eluded his hunters, Rambo slips back into the town, which he then proceeds to destroy. Cornered in the sheriff's office, his old commanding officer, Colonel Trautman, attempts to talk him into surrendering. In this final confrontational scene the normally reticent Rambo blurts out all the things that have been eating away at him since his return from Vietnam. The catalyst for Rambo's diatribe comes when Trautman tells him that it's all over:

> Nothing is over, nothing! You don't just turn it off. It wasn't my war—you asked me, I didn't ask you—and I did what I had to do to win. But somebody wouldn't let us win. Then I came back to the world and I see all those maggots at the airport, protesting me, spitting on me, calling me a baby killer and all kinds of vile crap . . .

Back there I could fly a gunship, I could drive a tank, I was in charge of million-dollar equipment. Back here I can't even hold down a job parking cars . . . Back here there's nothing!

In this final speech, Rambo touches on all of the revisionist biases, central to which is the notion that the war was lost at home, not in the field; that the government, having called the likes of Rambo to war, held the military back from winning; that the peace movement (positioned as a present-day version of "commie dupes") undermined America from within; and that a confused and dispirited nation then turned its back on the "real victims" of the war, the American veterans.

By the time the sequel, *Rambo: First Blood II*, was released in 1985, the outline of a strident conservative populism had become evident in Vietnam War films. In the sequel, the notion that the war was lost because of home-front back stabbing is joined to the controversy over the possibility that American soldiers missing in action (MIAs) are still being held captive in Southeast Asia. In *Uncommon Valor* (1983), *Missing in Action* (1984), *Missing in Action II* (1985), *P.O.W.: The Escape* (1986), and the second Rambo vehicle, the quest to free MIAs follows a similar scenario: in spite of presumably conclusive proof that prisoners do indeed exist in Vietnam, the U.S. government is unwilling to act because of pending diplomatic and trade agreements in the area. It is thus left up to various individuals, invariably portrayed as former Green Berets, to go back into Vietnam and bring the prisoners out. And this they achieve in the face of overwhelming odds and despite the attempts of U.S. government agencies to stop them. In effect, these portrayals of an intractable masculinity that refuses to accept the cultural terms of defeat, and that must continually return to the historic site of its castration, amounts to more than a simple case of revisionism, for what is at stake in these narratives appears to be the desire to recover the once-unquestioned power of the warrior male.

That this desire is deeply rooted in public fantasy, as well as in military institutions and in the bonds that are formed in the war experience itself, is demonstrated in *Uncommon Valor.* Here the motivation to refight the war stems from a fractured sense of oedipal guilt, in which a father (a former Marine colonel played by Gene Hackman) assembles and retrains a team of Vietnam veterans in an effort to rescue his son from a Vietnamese work camp. The veterans, all but one of whom had served with the son, are also motivated by a sense of lingering guilt because they had been unable to stop the capture in the first place. This oedipal theme is reinforced by the presence of a younger man (Patrick Swayze) who, although too young to have fought in Vietnam, is allowed to join the team because he is seeking to avenge his father's death in Vietnam. Thus the heritage of a militarized masculinity—the ultimate patriarchal currency of the all-male group—is what must be regained and valorized in *Uncommon Valor.* The bonds forged between soldiers in combat are equated with the bond between fathers and sons (mothers are completely missing from this equation), and in many ways Hackman's character is set up not just as the leader of the group but as its father. Set against him are the politicians who, Hackman explains, "never lost a single son in Vietnam" and who are incapable of understanding the purely paternal drives of the warrior male. Such politicians, in other words, are incapable of forging the necessary militarized subject/sons; they have failed in the business of reproducing the armored masculinity of war—a theme I will return to shortly.

Another variation on the MIA theme appeared with the release of *The Hanoi Hilton* (1987), a film that deals with the plight of captured airmen held prisoner in North Vietnam during the war. Again, the characters in this film locate the real enemy back home in the form of peace activism and a supposedly liberal media, both of which are undermining a perfectly winnable war. It is that motif that marks the major ideological claim of the Vietnam War films of the 1980s: the war could have been won but for certain groups and political interests, which tied the hands of the American fighting man. Thus, shortly before he returns to Vietnam in search of MIAs in *First Blood II,* Rambo poses the question, "Are they going to let us win this time?" The real question, however, is, Who precisely are "they"? The list of potential candidates for what one commentator terms the "stab in the back stakes" include the "media, the politicians, the bureaucrats, the pointy-headed intellectuals, Jane Fonda, the hippies, the bleeding heart liberals, the pansy pacifists, Congress, the State Department and even . . . the C.I.A."[45] And one can add to that list the higher echelon of the military command, the members of which are often shown to be more concerned with their personal careers than with events taking place on the battlefield.

In the second Rambo film, this overdetermined "they" is embodied in the figure of Murdock, the operations chief who is responsible for Rambo's mission. In sharp contrast to the stripped-down jungle-fighting Rambo, who spends much of the film armed with just a bowie knife and a bow and arrow, Murdock is ensconced in an air-conditioned command-and-control center surrounded by banks of computers, radar screens, and satellite communications technology. Moreover, Murdock's mission is not to locate and rescue POWs, as Rambo believes, but to placate public opinion and head off congressional investigations by proving that there are no American prisoners in Vietnam. Thus, when Rambo actually finds American captives and attempts to bring one back with him, Murdock abandons him to the Vietnamese army and their Soviet advisors. Murdock, then, in contrast to Rambo's self-willed version of the residual frontier ethic, is a political version of the "other-directed" corporate man—a willing subject of the military-industrial complex and its hidden agenda.

The 1980s Vietnam War films thus identify no specific home-front enemy. Instead, the enemy is a hodgepodge of elements spanning, on the one hand, the liberal-left continuum in American life and, on the other, the faceless bureaucrats of the military-industrial complex. In the end, as Russell Berman insists, the dramatic tension of such films "derives less from the conflict with Communism . . . than from the conflict between the soldier hero and the American military bureaucracy: Rambo as the supply-side fighter."[46]

Internal domestic and institutional antagonisms, not external threats to the national order, motivate the new generation of avenging superheroes.

This spate of revisionist films on the war accounts in large part for the extremely popular reception, both with critics and with audiences, of Oliver Stone's *Platoon* (1986). Indeed, *Platoon* was not only hailed by the critics as a welcome antidote to such films as *Rambo* and *Missing in Action* but was also received by most audiences as the first film of the 1980s to deal with the real war.[47] The realistic effect of *Platoon*—its attempt to represent the terror and the numbing confusion of daily battle—was almost uniformly cited as its primary virtue. According to *Time*, Oliver Stone was showing us "the way it really was."[48] David Halberstam, who reviewed the film for the *New York Times*, wrote that *Platoon* "exists only, as they say, in-country. It has no other objective, no other agenda. . . . It is painfully realistic."[49] Or, as one ex-marine has put it, *Platoon* gives us "the grunt's-eye-view" of the war.[50]

Certainly *Platoon* aspires to engage its audience in the painful reality of the war. But it would be wrong to see it as simply a "realistic" version of the war, as so many commentators have claimed, particularly given its melodramatic polarization of good and evil in the characters of Sergeant Elias and Sergeant Barnes. Still, *Platoon* produces an effect of the real, not in its images per se, but rather in the manner in which it engages its audience. The extremely long final battle scene, for instance, is indebted to *Apocalypse Now* and other stylized representations of war. And yet in its very duration the scene gives the spectator a glimpse of the confusion of war and a feeling of the utter helplessness and vulnerability of the average grunt. The film reproduces—for a limited duration of screen time rather than the extended duration of an actual tour of duty—the experience of being caught up in war. The "look" of the Vietnam War in film was reestablished on a different plane with the release of *Platoon*, and the measure of the success of this new aesthetic of war can be judged by the speed at which it moved directly to television in the shape of the series *Tour of Duty*.

The Vietnam War, as it had been constructed in films from the late 1970s to the mid-1980s, had come to be understood as an American Waterloo—a tragic wasting of ideals, lives, and materials in a cause that had been invested from the start with the overdrawn rhetoric of melodrama and even hysteria. The stylistic excesses of *Apocalypse Now* and the sensationalist excesses of *Rambo: First Blood II* work from within just this set of received dramatic possibilities and structures of feeling. The changes that *Platoon* worked on the received conventions were not so much at the level of style as at the level of narrative content—specifically in its detailed examination of the psychosocial microcosm of the infantry platoon. In this, its overall political effects went no further than previous films about the war simply because the focus remained fixed on the individual. The relevant historical and political details of American involvement in Vietnam are no more addressed in *Platoon* than in previous cinematic attempts to reimagine the war. Thus *Platoon* signaled not the arrival of novel formal or stylistic qualities within the subgenre of Vietnam combat films but rather the emergence of a new emphasis or concern with content.

Platoon's attention to the hitherto ignored banalities of the combat experience, coupled with its intense focus on the deeply divided American forces that fought the singularly determined Vietnamese, was understood to open new vistas on what the combat veterans of the war had been through. But in its formal and conceptual structures *Platoon* remained caught within what Colin MacCabe has theorized as the "classic realist film text"—a narrative form that hinges on private, personal dramas, while supressing wider social or political dimensions.[51] While *Platoon* revealed something new about the everyday of the Vietnam War (in the context of the mid-1980s), it never attempted to go beyond the immediate experience to demonstrate how the war was the effect of specific political and economic motivations that were deeply embedded in the domestic power structures of the United States.

In this regard, it is important to stress that *Platoon* engages

its audience (an audience imagined to be male) in a contradictory position vis-à-vis the war. On the one hand, it aes-
theticizes the war and romanticizes the experience of the all-
male group composed of soldiers of various racial, class, and
regional backgrounds. In this way, *Platoon* adapts some of
the conventions of the traditional World War II combat film,
and in the process it substitutes a vision of national unity in
the face of otherwise insurmountable differences (particularly of race, but also certainly of class).[52] The split within the
platoon—between the "heads" led by Elias and the "straights"
led by Barnes—is a self-reflexive divide between the cinematic conventions of the post–World War II era and those of
the post-1960s. The great divide between the two halves of
the platoon is, in effect, not a matter of politics but of historical style. An emergent sixties sensibility, which is played
out in terms of music (acid rock and Motown—an integrated
musical backdrop that also signals the racial mix of the group),
pot smoking, and self-expression, is set off against the residual masculine codes of the previous period, pictured in terms
of bourbon, country-and-western music, poker, and a posturing machismo.

   In its portrayal of the "heads," on the other hand, *Platoon*
presents an alternative view of war that extends the conventions of the traditional war film in its vision of male bonding
outside of a heroic masculinity. At one point in the film, for
instance, after the protagonist, Chris Taylor (Charlie Sheen),
has been initiated into the pot-smoking rituals of the "head's"
underground club, the soldiers wind up dancing together in
a moment of rare intimacy and friendship. This kind of scene
would not have been possible in the war films of the 1940s or
1950s (except as comic relief), and it certainly serves to contest
the image of the lone figure of Rambo, whose masculinity is
predicated on a virtually pathological individualism. It is perhaps for this reason that the film garnered so much critical
attention, given the suppression of that alternative vision of
male identity in contemporary American culture. Having
said that, however, these scenes of male bonding, as the film
makes clear, are temporary triumphs won in the face of

national antagonisms of race and class that the soldiers carried with them to Vietnam. As much as *Platoon* speaks to forms of male friendship otherwise missing in mainstream Hollywood films, it also reveals a deeply divided sense of national identity and purpose, which the war and its aftermath engendered.

With the release of *Platoon* the American cinema had entered a new phase of reconstructing the war in Vietnam. It had discovered a more gritty and realist route to box office success and to what is, in effect, war profiteering. *Platoon* also demonstrated that filmmakers no longer need obsess unduly over the political implications of Vietnam, given that a usable past was now available in the codes set forth by Oliver Stone. That this was probably not Stone's intention is beside the point, although it might explain why he was so determined to get Ron Kovic's more critical assessment of the war and American culture, *Born on the Fourth of July*, onto film. The spectacle of masculinity at war—shot through with the melodramatic tropes of male rivalry and an oedipalized rites of passage, and concluding with a nod in the direction of the tragic waste of it all—would now, in the late 1980s, become the conventional way of constructing the Vietnam War in American culture.

Paul Fussell, then, is correct when he observes that the grim actualities of the Vietnam War have resisted being turned into a "Disneyfied" musical. Musicals conventionally celebrate achieved identities and resolvable desires—the constituent structures of a romantic subjectivity generally missing from Vietnam representations. Chris Taylor, for example, in spite of his rite of passage, leaves the war without a stable sense of male identity. He describes himself as "an orphan of war; a child born of two fathers who was now abandoned to his fate." The two fathers, Barnes and Elias, have been killed off (Chris himself having murdered Barnes), leaving Chris to ponder his future in terms of those disparate patriarchs "fighting for possession of my soul." In this way, most of the Vietnam War films deal in a different dramatic currency from the musical, namely, the tragic excesses of melodrama.

Musicals and melodramas occupy opposite ends of the dramatic spectrum—or as one film scholar puts the case, melodramas are "musicals turned inside out." Melodrama thus becomes the perfect dramatic vehicle for realizing the war experience, "when the dream changes into nightmare, when desire becomes obsession, and the creative will turns into mad frenzy."[53] Nightmare states, thwarted desires, and obsessive frenzy are the recurring tropes of Vietnam War dramas in both film and television, particularly in the latter half of the 1980s. At the center of many of these representations, from *Coming Home* through *China Beach* to *Born on the Fourth of July,* resides a tangle of emotional issues that are ultimately worked through a mise-en-scène that owes less to the battlefield than to the conventions of domestic and family melodrama.

5

MELODRAMATIC EXCESS: THE BODY IN/OF THE TEXT

The Men and Women Who Served In Vietnam
Were Also Heroes. We Just Didn't Realize It Then.
CHINA BEACH RETURNS
ADVERTISEMENT IN *TV GUIDE*, 1–7 JUNE 1991

THE *TV GUIDE* advertisement for the return of the television series *China Beach* in the summer of 1991 quoted above is indicative of the ways in which the Vietnam War has been reclaimed and rewritten in the light of the Persian Gulf War. That rewriting involves the resurrection of certain kinds of heroes—those who served—at the expense of an all-inclusive "we." In this context, "we" means "the people," those of us who refused to recognize and celebrate the heroic sacrifices of the Vietnam War veterans. The proposition that "we" somehow managed to dictate to the media managers and politicians a policy of silence and neglect fails to connect with lived experience, where veterans and "the people" are in fact one and the same. Still, that failure does not alter the pervasive and structuring ideology that messages such as these have come to form within the present-day politics of media discourse.

After several months in hiatus, basically the period of the Gulf War, *China Beach* returned for what *TV Guide* called "one last hurrah . . . a wistful, bittersweet episode that finds McMurphy [Dana Delany] serving as the maid of honor at a wedding." In the event, the wedding, set in 1983, turned out to be a vehicle for a series of flashbacks aimed at resolving plot complications from the previous season. Those complications for the most part involved romance and marriage between individuals whose military rank or class position suggested a fundamental incompatibility. And although it is clear that those liaisons had been made in a time of war (war as the leveler of classes?), at no time did the war itself make an appearance. In point of fact, if anything marked the narrative development of *China Beach* across the seasons, it was the gradual erasure of overt references to, or representations of, the show's larger setting—the Vietnam War. That erasure resulted in an emphasis on romantic and melodramatic motifs at the expense of the larger political story of America's involvement in Vietnam. Consequently, narrative lines that, at least occasionally, suggested that more was at stake in Vietnam than simply the dating practices of nurses and doctors tended to disappear into the background as *China Beach* became virtually indistinguishable from other television series concerned with romance and family drama.

China Beach, however, is not a singular example of the favoring of melodrama over more incisive forms of political and cultural analysis. As I suggested in chapter 4, the representational terrain of the Vietnam War that has evolved over the past two decades reveals a tendency to represent events in terms of male fantasies, rivalries, and anxieties—the psychosocial elements that have long been the standard fare of melodrama. What is significant about this tendency in *China Beach* is that the series was initially concerned to "bring the war home" to a different audience, namely, women. But that original project to restore women's experience to the history of the Vietnam War faltered under the dual pressures of political events (from the invasion of Panama to the Gulf War) and the dictates of the "ratings war" (which resulted in increased interference from network managers who were concerned to "lighten up" the series).[1] Consequently, *China Beach* moved increasingly into the realm of soap opera, where the Vietnam War became merely a convenient backdrop for romantic action.

China Beach epitomizes the changes in perception and reception of the war that have taken place in recent history—a history in which the texts of Vietnam have been opened up to multiple inscriptions. Unlike earlier Vietnam War films, which focused on a single male soldier (whether empowered or impaired), *China Beach* disperses both the gaze and the narrative interest across a variety of characters and a multitude of plot lines. Here, excessive representation extends beyond the body as figure to the body as text. In other words, if the return of the repressed in earlier Vietnam War films finds its clearest and most hyperbolic representation in the heroic male body of war, in *China Beach* that return involves the body of the text entirely, where what is repressed at the level of narrative reemerges in music and mise-en-scène. Hence, the focus is no longer simply the body in the text, but rather the text as body—as a corpus of signs and meanings.

None of this, of course, is separable from contemporary politics, which have repositioned and remilitarized subjectivities to such an extent that the spectacle of the Persian Gulf War quite quickly, and easily, saturated the entire cultural field. Thus, in spite of the often contradictory messages in many Vietnam War texts, the male body as spectacle and site of excess ultimately collapses into patriotic display. That collapse is certainly true of the Rambo films, and it has come to characterize, to an even greater extent, the war's return to television in the series *Tour of Duty* and *China Beach.*

What I am arguing here, then, is that the discourses of war and the cultural construction of certain kinds of subjectivities and bodies are closely related. Before a nation can go to war, it must have in place the necessary bodies, the armored and militarized bodies, upon which to inscribe the designs of war, and through which war can be imagined, read, and desired. To say this is to recognize that the body is acted upon and constructed in culture and that, furthermore, there is a history to that process. Not only has the body "been perceived, interpreted, and represented differently in different epochs, but it has also been lived differently . . . subjected to various technologies and means of control, and incorporated into different rhythms of production and consumption, pleasure and pain."[2]

The insights informing this historical perspective were developed by Michel Foucault, whose work on the emergence of a politics of the body has influenced subsequent thinking on the subject. Foucault's history of the political administration of bodies demonstrates that the increasingly calculated management of life was brought into being by new forms of state power—what Foucault terms collectively "bio-power." Beginning in the seventeenth century, the human body itself came to be seen as an instrument and as a site for the inscription of the needs of the state. Consequently, the body came to be increasingly thought of as a machine assigned to the institutions of the state to be disciplined, controlled, and made passive, that it might be integrated more effectively into the emerging regimentation of industrial production within a predominantly urban existence. As Foucault argues, capitalism "would not have been possible without the controlled insertion of bodies into the machinery of production and the adjustment of the phenomena of populations to economic processes."[3] Moreover, the capitalist nation-states that came to dominate the world would not have been able to do so without, on the one hand, the new industrial technologies of war and, on the other, the new disciplinary techniques that produced the necessary militarized subjectivities and bodies of war.

Foucault might have seen Stanley Kubrick's *Full Metal Jacket* (1987) as a depiction of military discipline's intent to produce an "instrumental coding of the body" so as to forge "a body weapon, body tool, body machine complex."[4] The opening sequences portray in excruciating detail the mechanistic deconstruction of social identities and the reconstruction of depersonalized military subjects during marine training. *Full Metal Jacket* thereby offers a more critical view of the military experience than *Platoon*, since the latter concludes on an ahistorical and mythical note, elevating war to the level of a timeless struggle between good and evil that is beyond the control of mere humans. Kubrick, on the other hand, insists that wars, like the people who fight them, are historically and politically constructed. His film reveals that gender and war, and specifically masculinity and the military body, are not naturally occurring phenomena but the specific result of historical and cultural processes.

This general proposition has attracted the attention of feminist scholars working in related areas, who have extended Foucault's observations in order to deconstruct the cultural norms of sexuality and gender, which have come to establish themselves as essential biological truths. As Judith Butler has written, "the body can be theorized as a cultural site of gender meaning . . . operating within a network of entrenched cultural norms." Against the assumption that gender is the result of biological determinism, Butler insists on gender as a social and cultural construct that emerges from a "network of gender determinations fixed in a dialectic between culture and choice." The choice, however, to assume a certain kind of body, to live or wear one's body a certain way, implies "a world of already established corporeal styles." Thus the dialectic between culture and choice involves an already established cultural reality that is "laden with sanctions, taboos and proscriptions."[5]

In appropriating these ideas for an analysis of the military body in recent American history, I should add that the production of military bodies is an extension of the production of male subjectivity more generally. In American culture the military body has traditionally been a valorized body, presented and represented for social consumption as a natural and useful project for young men to take up. That presentation is not so much of corporeal styles as of *the* corporeal style—an ideological body style that is positioned within those legitimizing discourses that underwrite and extend the power of the state. The military body is thus sanctioned as a national asset to be displayed within the spectacle of politics and celebrated in every conceivable media format.

If we can accept the notion of a system of cultural production that sets the terms of a dialectic between body styles, genders, and embedded social norms, then it follows that in times of social stress and cultural crisis, such as the Vietnam War era, this dialectic will become at least partially dysfunctional. More to the point, in the aftermath of events such as a lost war, problems will arise in the cultural and political project of producing and valorizing militarized bodies and subjectivities. Cultural crises and breakdowns such as those surrounding a lost war, then, are capable of causing a disturbance in the sphere of sexuality and sexual identity.[6] In this sense, the lost war in Vietnam compromised the hegemonic certainties of the Cold War period, when national interest and personal desire were to a large extent interwoven, and initiated a process of disassembling and reassembling the symbolic military body in American culture.

At the level of cinematic representations, we can trace a history of the shifting productions and perceptions of the military body: for example, from the idealized military figures portrayed by John Wayne in the 1940s and 1950s, to the 1970s, when the military body was portrayed as crippled or verging on psychosis. Jon Voight's paraplegic veteran in *Coming Home* is perhaps the best-known example, but there are many more: Dennis Hopper in *Tracks* (1977), Henry Winkler in *Heroes* (1977), Nick Nolte in *Who'll Stop the Rain* (1978), and John Heard in *Cutter's Way* (1981) all represented the breakdown of the military body. Even in such box office successes as *The Deer Hunter* and *Apocalypse Now* the experience of war, no longer a final heroic tuning of masculinity, produces addiction, paralysis, and a loss of male confidence and authority. And in Marlon Brando's portrayal of the once-ideal soldier Colonel Kurtz, the soldier's body of war has become bloated on violence to the point of satiety and madness.

Representations of war and the military body underwent further changes in the mid-1980s, as Hollywood returned to more traditional forms of the combat genre. Such films as *Platoon* and *Hamburger Hill* (1987) and the television series

Tour of Duty announced a new cycle of war films promising a more sympathetic view of soldiering in Vietnam. This is not to say that those productions are simply an unproblematic return of the same; indeed, while they have opened the way for a new round of military spectacles and patriotic backslapping, they have not entirely suppressed critical themes. (As I noted earlier, even the Rambo films contain populist and critical themes.) Those productions, along with such others as *Purple Hearts* (1984), *Full Metal Jacket, Good Morning, Vietnam* (1987), and *China Beach*, indicate that the war in Vietnam has become invested with a range of melodramatic and tragicomic elements that signal the opening up of this once-taboo subject to multiple textual inscriptions. As melodrama has come to dominate combat films and television shows, narrative focus has shifted from the tragic effects of a botched foreign policy on the individual soldier to the interactions among a group of soldiers, with the war as an exotic backdrop.

The turn to melodrama was noted, albeit obliquely, in Roger Corliss's review of *Platoon* in *Time* magazine, which noted that the soldiers in Vietnam "re-created the world back home. . . . The Viet Cong and North Vietnamese Army were shadowy figures in this family tragedy; stage center, it was sibling rivalry."[7] Similar terms litter the critical responses to Vietnam War films; for example, Auster and Quart describe Hollywood's attempts to contain the "real" experience and conditions of the war "within the confines of romantic soap opera and heroic melodrama." They go on to suggest that a desire to reduce historical experience to established Hollywood formulas is typical of American commercial filmmaking in general, and that there is little hope of a more accurate rendering of war so long as Hollywood sticks to its tried and tested "fantasies and stereotypes." The best we can look for are those moments of breakthrough that stem not from the intentions of filmmakers but from the processes of reception—that is, when the images themselves awaken the "memory of an actual event" and "suggest something of the harrowing quality of that experience."[8] Meanwhile, the pressure to confine the war experience within the structures of melodrama is likely to shape most representations of the Vietnam War.

That films dealing with the Vietnam War are approached by critics in terms of their melodramatic affects and effects is, on the face of it, somewhat surprising. Although the term *melodrama* has been notoriously unstable in film studies ("a fragmented generic category," as Christine Gledhill calls it)[9] and, since the 1970s, has been attached to a complex array of film genres, it has generally been exempted from use in the study of films in which the action is exterior, such as the Western, gangster, and action-adventure film. In those films the protagonist's search for an oedipal identity usually involves the conquering of the setting itself. Melodrama, on the other hand, has been associated with interior space, with the domestic sphere of family and private reflection, where the externalization of psychological states is magnified in the music and in certain elements of the mise-en-scène. Moreover, film melodramas have been organized around the crucial tropes of pathos and irony, as well as the alienation brought about by failed familial or sexual relationships. Geoffrey Nowell-Smith describes the contours of this particular aspect of the family melodrama:

> What is at stake . . . is the survival of the family unit and the possibility for individuals of acquiring an identity which is also a place within the system, a place in which they can both be "themselves" and "at home," in which they can simultaneously enter, without contradiction, the symbolic order and bourgeois society. It is a condition of the drama that the attainment of such a place is not easy and does not happen without sacrifice, but it is rare for it to be seen as radically impossible.[10]

When melodrama features a male character as its protagonist, the narrative often traces a failed oedipal trajectory and the consequent problems of achieving a stable patriarchal identity. Frequently the protagonist suffers from "an impairment of his masculinity—at least in contrast to the

mythic potency of the hero of the Western."[11] Still, melodrama is not exclusively about "either the family or individual psychology"; rather, it exteriorizes conflict and psychic structures in a process that aims to produce a melodrama
of psychology.[12] In other words, the general work of melodramatic conventions and structures is not necessarily concerned with "the release of individual repression" so much
as it is with the "public enactment of socially unacknowl-
edged states."[13] Extending this argument into the debate
between the different functions of realism and melodrama,
Gledhill suggests that whereas realism usually assumes that
"the world is capable of both adequate explanation and representation," melodrama offers no such confidence. On the
contrary, much like the condensed and displaced cinematic
presentations of the Vietnam War, melodrama "attests to
forces, desires, [and] fears which, though no longer granted
metaphysical reality, nevertheless appear to operate in human life independently of rational explanation." That emphasis on the irrational, Gledhill concludes, is a mark of "melodrama's search for something lost, inadmissable, repressed,"
binding melodrama "to an atavistic past."[14] And that description is an accurate portrayal of what the media spectacles of
the Vietnam War are about.

For years the war was repressed in American culture, and
those who fought in it were, upon their return, condemned
to silence, forced to internalize the defeat as personal psychological trauma. Throughout the 1970s Vietnam veterans
seemed to stalk the culture like a bad conscience, the living
reminders of a conflict that some saw as a struggle between
the forces of good and evil—the terms being politically
reversible depending on the opinion of the user—and that
others saw as an eruption of atavistic tendencies that had
now been finally laid to rest. Thus, when the war finally
reentered the popular consciousness by means of the mass
media, realist representational modes tended to be elided in
favor of the melodramatic.

When we take the terms of these arguments, then, and
join them with the remarks in the review of *Platoon*, men-

tioned above, we can begin to identify a structural topography in the various representations of the Vietnam War in
American culture that draw upon the traditional terrain of
melodrama. That topography becomes all the more obvious
when we recall that *melodrama* originally denoted drama
set to music (*melos*). If a single distinction marks Vietnam
War films from films about previous American wars, it is the
special place accorded to the musical soundtrack. No film
about the Vietnam War seems quite complete without a
1960s rock'n'roll accompaniment; perhaps beginning with
Coming Home, no moment of pathos, tragedy, or reflection
is allowed to pass that has not been amplified by a significant selection from the popular music of the period. This by-
now-established convention of Vietnam War films has been
appropriated wholesale by television treatments of the subject. In *China Beach*, for example, music and performance
were a regular feature of each week's show. Thus moments of
intense feeling were usually emotionally amplified either by
the musical soundtrack or through one or more of the characters performing a suitably charged rendering of a contemporary popular song. Indeed, during the series's first six weeks,
one of the central female characters was a professional pop
singer whose career became entangled with the daily dramas of the combat casualty hospital.

That certain kinds of 1960s popular music have come to
signify an important emotional dimension of the American
war in Vietnam is also attested to by *Good Morning, Vietnam*. In that film the music itself becomes a contested site of
popular meanings within the larger terrain of the war. The
combatants in that contest are an Armed Forces Radio disc
jockey, played by Robin Williams, who is versed in the popular tastes and cultural needs of the G.I.s, and the out-of-touch
army officers who run the radio station and who demand
a quieter, presixties, format. In their confrontations, music
comes to stand in for the more pressing historical drama of
class and race that is played out between careerist officers,
removed from the daily terrors of the war, and the combat
grunts who would rather fight the war to the accompani-

ment of Jimi Hendrix than Mantovani. The film's appropriation of period music is at some level an attempt to conjure up
an authentic sense of what Raymond Williams has called an
era's "structures of feeling"; at another level, however, it represents a profitable media tie-in and further emphasizes the
attempt to adapt the Vietnam War to basic melodramatic
conventions.

Until the recent spate of Vietnam War films, *Coming Home*
offered what was perhaps the most constant use of music to
underline a war film's basic melodramatic structures. The
protagonist, a paraplegic war veteran named Luke Martin
(Jon Voight), is first introduced as a violently bitter and frustrated victim of both the war itself and of the pre-Vietnam
cultural determinants of American masculinity that caused
him to desire heroic participation in the war in the first place.
Consequently, Luke is having a difficult time accepting the
physical results of his tour of duty in Vietnam. Instead of
providing Luke with a traditionally celebrated passage into
male adulthood, the war has in fact arrested his oedipal trajectory, at least temporarily, at the level of an unstable psychological state that swings wildly between childish aggression and passive resignation.

It is during Luke's confinement in the hospital that he
meets Sally Hyde (Jane Fonda). Sally, too, is a product of pre-
Vietnam cultural and psychological modes and is initially
portrayed as a passive and deferring military wife. With her
husband, Bob (Bruce Dern), now in Vietnam, however, Sally
is forced to move into civilian housing, where there is less
pressure to conform to the proprieties and proscriptions of
life on the military base. Encouraged by a friend, Sally volun-
teers for part-time work at the VA hospital, where contact
with the disabled veterans begins to open her eyes to previously invisible aspects of the war in Vietnam. Moreover, as
the world outside of the confines of the marine base im-
presses itself on Sally, she begins to change and to question
her former attachments and assumptions. These psychological shifts are registered in her changing dress and hairstyle,
which reflect the free-flowing fashion of the era. Sally also

becomes more spontaneous and independent in her behavior and is eventually drawn into having an affair with Luke.

At this stage of the narrative, Luke's initial anger and resentment have been tempered somewhat as he becomes increasingly mobile, first in a wheelchair and then in a specially customized car. No longer violent and unpredictable, Luke emerges as a sensitive and even nurturing character whose psychological and political determinants now lean toward passivism. As a male protagonist, however, his weakness and paralysis have, in effect, moved him outside the traditional cinematic codes of assertive masculine subjectivity. In *The Remasculinization of America* Susan Jeffords sums up Luke's progression:

> His physical weakness . . . is foregrounded throughout the film as a nonthreatening posture in sharp contrast to the stiff-backed soldiers who still believe in war. And although his actions toward the end of the film . . . indicate a strength and decisiveness, this strength is clearly a nonviolent and passive one. . . . The price of his release from the hospital was his gradual containment of this anger and violence, now effectively neutralized (feminized/castrated). And Luke's increasingly feminine . . . characteristics parallel his growing expression of blame for his activities in the war.[15]

Luke and Sally, then, are able to change and readjust previously held beliefs in the light of present experience; they are shown to be capable of casting off the constricting remnants of their former selves. And although the process introduces moments of psychological and sexual instability and stress, they do manage to acquire (or reacquire) identities that are, to quote Nowell-Smith again, "a place in which they can both be 'themselves' and 'at home.' "

Bob, on the other hand, is incapable of change and continues to be pathologically locked into male fantasies of a heroic manhood that can only be legitimated on the battlefield. It is this pathology, moreover, that ultimately leads to Bob's suicide following the disillusionments and confusions of Vietnam. In ways that turn out to be more disabling than Luke's experiences, Bob discovers that the Vietnam War, instead of providing a proving ground for a heroic masculinity, has instead totally undermined his sense of identity. His discovery of Sally's affair with the crippled Luke merely adds to his already intense feelings of dislocation; it is clear that the war itself has irrevocably violated all of the masculine fantasies that Bob desired in and for himself.

Although the war in Vietnam is not directly represented in *Coming Home*, it has, nevertheless, an enabling textual function in pointing to an unspeakable experience. When Sally asks Bob to tell her what it's like in Vietnam, for example, he is unable to articulate a response at first. Eventually he is able to blurt out: "It's in my head and I can't get it out. I don't know what it's like, I only know what it is. TV shows what it's like . . . it sure as hell don't show what it is." Vietnam is thus literally unspeakable in *Coming Home*. It cannot be, to quote Gledhill, "granted metaphysical reality"; it is a structuring absence that can be made legible only through the exteriorization of Luke's passivity and Bob's psychic stress.

That process of exteriorization is given further expression through the soundtrack, which must stand in for the inability of ordinary language to articulate Bob's deteriorating state of mind. An increasingly frenetic soul number (the Chambers Brothers' "Time Has Come Today") guides the spectator through the buildup to Bob's emotionally explosive confrontation with Sally over her affair with Luke. The confrontation takes place in the living room, where the television set becomes a suggestive prop for Bob to lean his assault rifle on. Luke arrives in time to defuse the situation and to talk Bob out of any further violence. In the process, Luke also disarms Bob and, while Sally attempts to comfort her husband, very deliberately unloads the rifle and retracts the extended bayonet. Bob, too, is thus neutralized, and his symbolic castration is now complete. The war has irreversibly altered the gendered determinants of both Luke's and Bob's sense of masculine identity. For the rest of the film, the only remaining signifier of Bob's former male status is his marine captain's uniform—and in effect, the uniform merely points to the absence within, the lack that cannot be acknowledged in language. Finally, with the soundtrack again articulating Bob's traumatized and unstable state, this time through a quiet folk song ("Once I Was a Soldier"), he symbolically removes his uniform, dog tags, and Sally's ring, and swims out into the final embrace of the "Great Mother Ocean."

Coming Home is not the only example of how melodramatic conventions were used to represent the Vietnam War experience in the late 1970s. *Taxi Driver, Tracks, Heroes, Who'll Stop the Rain,* and *The Deer Hunter* all present a crisis in male subjectivity that is then acted out within the domestic arena. In the changed cultural and political conditions of the 1980s, however, a different range of discourses, media representations, and public spectacles of healing came to constitute the psychological and emotional terrain of the war. As I have already noted, the American cinema's approach to the Vietnam War is stretched between Ramboesque fantasies, on the one hand, and the claims to realism of *Platoon* and *Hamburger Hill,* on the other. Somewhere in between stand the dark comedies of *Full Metal Jacket* and *Good Morning Vietnam.* In 1989 these were joined by the emotionally pitched *Casualties of War* and the family melodrama of *In Country.* But perhaps one of the most unlikely sources for a melodramatic rendering of the effects of the Vietnam War is the film version of Ron Kovic's uncompromisingly angry memoir *Born on the Fourth of July* (1990). Even more surprisingly, it was adapted to the screen and directed by Oliver Stone, himself an angry veteran whose political sympathies matched Kovic's.

In the film version of *Born on the Fourth of July,* Kovic's family home is given screen time well beyond that depicted in the memoir. This ensures that one of Kovic's major themes is moved to the center of the narrative; namely, that the family and its supporting institutions (religion, school, and sports, for example) represent sites where the cultural reproduction of subjectivities necessary for war takes place. The home is also, however, the place where the emotional and physical consequences of war are felt most intensely and played out in the most excessive and melodramatic of ways.

Having returned from the war after months of sloppy and even dangerous treatment in run-down VA hospitals, Kovic (Tom Cruise) must adjust to life in a wheelchair amid the familiar clutter of his family's home. Every object in the home, from school photographs to sports trophies to the Catholic crucifix on the living room wall, comes to express the growing anger, confusion, and alienation that Kovic cannot himself articulate. In one particularly overwrought scene, Kovic returns home late one night after a frustrating and drunken night out with some friends; immediately upon his entering the house, his pent-up emotions erupt violently. Unable to express himself through the once-familiar terms of patriotism and sacrifice that had marked his identity before the Vietnam War, and feeling alienated from the emergent cultural changes taking place within his own generation, Kovic lashes out at the everyday objects that clutter the family space. He rips the crucifix from the wall and attempts to smash everything that signifies the "atavistic past" of his former, pre-Vietnam self. This histrionic scene draws the entire family into its emotional vortex, including Kovic's somewhat ineffectual and distraught father and his hysterical mother, who ends up striking him in a fit of anger. The family and the home are thus literally destroyed: the domestic arena can no longer contain the psychological consequences of the Vietnam War.

Kovic's sense of self has been so altered by the war that he is forced outside cultural conventions to find himself and to be at home. He goes first to Mexico, where he attempts to settle into a debauched life-style at a beach resort set up for wounded veterans, and then to the antiwar movement, where he finds a political outlet for his bitterness and anger. The film's conclusion, however, returns to melodrama. Having achieved a new sense of identity as a spokesperson for antiwar veterans—"a place within the system" where he can be himself again and "at home"—Kovic wheels himself onto the speaker's platform at the Democratic party's 1976 convention. The soundtrack gradually shifts from the applause of well-wishers, interlaced with "welcome home, Ron," to the voice of his mother repeating lines from the beginning of the film: "I had a dream, Ron; you were speaking before a huge crowd of people and they were applauding you." The scene rewrites the antiwar movement in terms of the past and in relation to the family drama, at once restoring Ron's masculine identity and simultaneously fulfilling his mother's prophecy.

In the ongoing search for a usable range of dramatic forms deemed commensurate with the oft-claimed need to heal the wounds of the war, television has emerged as the most consistent and accessible site of Vietnam representations. Beginning in 1980 with *Magnum, P.I.* and quickly followed by *The A Team* in 1982, numerous action-adventure series portrayed heroes who were Vietnam veterans of one sort or another. A short list would include *Air Wolf, Miami Vice, T.J. Hooker, Simon and Simon, Rip Tide, Matt Helm,* and *The Equalizer.* Other shows, such as *Hill Street Blues, Barney Miller,* and *Trapper John, M.D.,* regularly featured one or more characters who were Vietnam veterans. At another level, television has also been instrumental in representing its own genealogy of American involvement in Vietnam. By rummaging in archives, a number of documentary series have attempted to stitch together a television history of the war. Videotapes of one such series are widely advertised as available for sale on an installment basis ("And you can own the Tet Offensive for just $4.99," the advertisement claims).

But it was the advent of the weekly Vietnam War dramas *Tour of Duty* in 1987 and *China Beach* in 1988 that attracted the most critical and popular attention. Set in a casualty evacuation station attached to a military beachside recreational center near Da Nang, *China Beach* provided multiple opportunities for creating dramatic tensions. One episode in particular merits special attention, both for its use of melodramatic conventions and for its overlay of those conventions with a hyperbolic, excessive patriotic sentiment.

Entitled "Independence Day," the episode focuses on three

major lines of action, which feature strikingly conventionalized (indeed, allegorical) figures: the romance between an American nurse, Colleen McMurphy, and a handsome French doctor, Girard; the interaction between a Vietnamese cleaning woman and a "Doughnut Dolly" who both claim national possession of the Declaration of Independence; and an altercation between K.C., an American prostitute ("officers only"), and a black mortician, Beckett, over the oppression and opportunity wrought by American capitalism. The stories are interwoven through the events of a single day (the Fourth of July), which is marked by the continuous downpour of monsoon rains. Not only does the rain underline moments of emotional conflict, but thunder and lightning also punctuate certain scenes with a sense of the Gothic.

The first and lengthiest narrative line to be developed involves Colleen and Girard and, among other things, sets up themes of cross-cultural conflict and misunderstanding. Girard appears unexpectedly at the base to invite Colleen to lunch and catches her in the act of eating American candy bars from a care package provided by the Doughnut Dolly. Colleen, caught off guard by his sudden appearance, is somewhat embarrassed to be seen with the heavy residue of a mudpack on her face. Nevertheless, the pair settle down to eat a casual lunch, composed of American junk food from the care package. Although the meeting is perfectly friendly at first, a remark from Girard, concerning the way Americans always "trail" their culture along behind them wherever they go, initiates a debate about the American presence in Vietnam and its political consequences. Colleen trots out the official line, which, though hackneyed, appears to be her heartfelt sentiment: "We are giving the Vietnamese an opportunity to decide their own destiny . . . freedom of choice." Girard responds by accusing Americans in general of having a far too simple understanding of such complex concepts as freedom, then continues with a history lesson on the thousand-year struggle of the Vietnamese to rid themselves of occupying armies. Girard views the American presence as simply another military occupation that will be inevitably defeated and driven away. Indeed, Girard goes on to link the American presence in Vietnam to an even larger political history of occupation: the "Romans in Palestine, the British in India . . . the Nazis!"

Their differences notwithstanding, in parting Girard invites Colleen to his house for dinner that night, an invitation that leaves her in a quandary over what the correct dress code might be for dinner with a Frenchman. In what has become an established motif in *China Beach*, Colleen turns to K.C., whose support and advice has become a matter of trust. In the scene that follows, Colleen is shown trying on one of K.C.'s body-hugging dresses, which strikes her as more of "a declaration of war" than a piece of clothing.

Thus dressed, Colleen arrives at Girard's impressive French colonial villa, only to find that dinner is to be casual. Instead of the expected show of French cuisine, dinner consists of American hot dogs (although on French bread). Moreover, not only is she overdressed for the occasion, but dinner turns out to be a family affair. Much to Colleen's surprise, Girard, who has been positioned in the series as a man with a mysterious past, has two Vietnamese children.

As the dinner proceeds with the children in attendance (the boy is wearing an American cowboy costume), the Independence Day theme reappears as Colleen and Girard argue about the relative political merits of the French and American revolutions. Girard attempts to quote the French revolutionary motto of liberty and equality, but before he can finish the sentence, Colleen interrupts and substitutes "the guillotine" in place of "fraternity." Girard immediately comes back with a quote from Thomas Paine that denigrates the American revolution as merely "a military exercise for the preservation of the bourgeoisie's property." Colleen, taken aback, can only ask in surprise, "Our Thomas Paine said that?" To which Girard adds, "Yours until you threw him away for being too revolutionary."

In a last determined effort to keep the flag flying, Colleen proclaims her allegiance: "I am not going to apologize for indoor plumbing and air-lifting ravioli halfway around the world. I might not get the big picture, but I can live where I please, I can do as I please, and I can think as I please. I'm an American, damn it!" Girard and the children respond by applauding with cries of "bravo." Before either adult can continue the argument into deeper political differences, however, the young boy asks Colleen if she knows Roy Rogers. Instead of replying, she sings "Happy Trails" (thus "trailing" American culture behind her), and everyone joins in. And so the scene ends, not with political debate, but with an example from America's ubiquitous popular culture, which seems to follow these characters wherever they go.

Eventually, Colleen and Girard are alone. Unsure of Colleen's feelings at this point, Girard says that he would understand if she wished to leave. Instead of leaving, however, Colleen approaches Girard and they begin to embrace and kiss, a moment of romance that is quickly punctured by a Vietnamese servant who, speaking in French, informs Girard of an emergency at the nearby convent. Colleen's and Girard's intercultural love affair now begins to take on elements of the Gothic, replete with flashing lightning, crashing thunder, and a madwoman in the attic. Although Colleen has no idea what the emergency consists of, she nevertheless insists on accompanying Girard to the convent. Upon their arrival a nun ushers them up a flight of stairs, with candles and lightning supplying an eerie ambience. At the top of the stairs is a mysterious room that houses one of Girard's former wives, a Vietnamese woman who was driven insane by the death of her and Girard's child.

Back at the base, the Doughnut Dolly and a Vietnamese cleaning woman take up the theme of confinement and independence in a different key. The Doughnut Dolly is attempting to memorize The Declaration of Independence in preparation for her part in the Fourth of July pageant. Obviously stirred by the reading, the Vietnamese woman interrupts with the question, "You know Ho Chi Minh?" Her query generates a dialogue between the two women, who both claim national possession of the same document. "That

is our Declaration of Independence," the Vietnamese woman
insists, "I have heard Ho Chi Minh say these words many
times on the radio, in the newspaper," while the American
woman contends that the words are those of Thomas Jefferson. Unlike the American woman, however, who is unsure of
the words of the declaration even as she reads them from a
prepared script, the Vietnamese woman can recite the document from memory. The suggestion here is that the American Declaration of Independence has been, through rote repetition, reduced to little more than a prop in an annual ritual
and thus drained of its revolutionary content. In the context
of the Vietnamese revolution, however, Ho Chi Minh's version
of the declaration provides powerful political motivation to
an embattled people. The story line concludes with the Vietnamese woman, now dressed up as George Washington,
reading the declaration during the Fourth of July celebrations
at the base.

The third narrative line is that involving K.C. and the black
mortician, Beckett. In typical opportunistic fashion, K.C. has
volunteered for the job of registering G.I.s for upcoming elec-
tions. For this she is being paid for each soldier registered. In
order to insure a good turnout, she commandeers Beckett's
mortuary and sets it up as a combination registration station
and nightclub, complete with free beer and blue movies.
When Beckett unexpectedly discovers this carnivalesque
scene, in a place where he had been attending to dead soldiers only hours before, he becomes enraged and demands
that the mortuary be cleared. K.C., however, is not so easily
dismissed, and in a show of machine politics she calls on the
soldiers to vote on whether to stay or leave. Beckett not only
loses the vote but, in the process, is also intimidated by the
all-white soldiers.

Later, Beckett confronts K.C. about the incident and also
about her stealing his files containing the names of all the
dead soldiers that have passed through his mortuary. Apparently, the graveyard vote is also worth money to K.C., an
instance of political corruption that reminds Beckett of the
political situation back home, where African Americans have

regularly been denied the vote. But his idealism and anger do not impress K.C., who also comes from the wrong side of the tracks. Indeed, her response is equally as impassioned as Beckett's: "America is not about democracy," she claims. "It's capitalism, cash, that's what makes America hum, and that's why I love it. In America a poor girl can be a queen." To this, Beckett can only reply, "I'll never stop believing in the other America." In a final frustrated gesture, Beckett tears up a roll of K.C.'s money and stalks out.

The three narrative lines are tentatively resolved within their separate contexts, but only the conclusion to the episode attempts to bring them together in a final, hyperbolic display of emotionality and patriotic sentiment. Undaunted by the rain, a group of American soldiers and nurses attempts to play softball in the downpour. Bob Dylan's "A Hard Rain's A-Gonna Fall" is heard on the soundtrack, as if to underscore the futility of their efforts and, indeed, as if to comment on the futility of the American occupation of Vietnam. Shots of Colleen and Girard in an embrace, and of the Vietnamese woman dressed as George Washington, are intercut with shots of the softball game (which now includes a friendly K.C. and Beckett). Almost imperceptibly, "A Hard Rain's A-Gonna Fall" is replaced by "The Battle Hymn of the Republic"; a massive display of fireworks, accompanying close-ups of the central characters, remains on the screen for some time until finally, mercifully, the concluding credits appear. Patriotic sentiment overwhelms and literally drowns out critical commentary, and Independence Day becomes inextricably bound up with a melodrama that operates simultaneously to expose and to cover over the contradictions of the war.

I began this study with an overview of the historical and theoretical continuities that constitute the cultural horizon of the Vietnam continuum. Part of that theoretical horizon, I have argued, is often indistinguishable now from the fashionable rubric of the postmodern. As a theoretical approach to culture and history, postmodernism embraces diverse political and intellectual positions that offer both enabling and disabling perspectives on the state of modern culture and social experience. Thus, on the one hand, postmodernism offers insights into the contemporary "structure of feeling" in which the sheer proliferation of mass cultural images does appear to have penetrated many aspects of lived experience. But on the other hand, there is an influential tendency in postmodernist theory to celebrate the ruptures, dispersions, and discontinuities of everyday life and to announce the absolute end of history. This enthusiastic embrace of the sometimes fractured nature of experience offers little in the way of a critical analysis of emergent forms of economic production, or of new cultural movements and political sensibilities in the modern world.

The Vietnam War, for example, is claimed by some postmodernists to be unknowable in any empirical sense and ambiguous and undecidable in its effects—a semiotic terrain without depths or boundaries. What remains as history within the general collapse of categories and principles is merely the uprooted and dispersed fragments of pop images and simulacra, the disconnected bricolage that litters the mass cultural rewriting of the war in film, music, and television. Lost in this approach is any sense of the counter-memory of a once active and radical political opposition, or of the continuing influence of that opposition in the present.

Rather than view postmodernism as a break with the past or with history, I have found it more useful to view postmodernism as a series of rewritings and rearticulations of historical movements and styles, as well as of contemporary experiences. Indeed, this latter aspect of the postmodern condition has been an informing principle throughout this book. In the aftermath of the Persian Gulf War (what CBS termed "The Showdown in the Gulf"), a war that was brought to us with the oft-repeated promise that it would "not be another Vietnam," the process of rewriting the recent past has taken on a decidedly hyperbolic cast. During every possible public occasion, and in every available mass medium, that promise was repeated ad nauseam by political leaders and media managers. Finally, when the war proved to be a relatively easy victory, a turkey shoot resembling an arcade video game, the triumph of the much-touted "new world order" was claimed to be the final and definitive destruction of the Vietnam syndrome.

To recall a theme from chapter 1, the term *Vietnam syndrome* refers, among other things, to the residual yet persistent public memory of the Vietnam War as "a brutal fraud" and "a lawless imperial adventure."[16] It was against that view of history, and that view of war as a corrupting fraud motivated by an imperialist agenda, that government leaders found it necessary to assure an uncertain public of the legitimacy of the Persian Gulf cause. It was, moreover, in recognition of that agenda that the antiwar movement's chant became "No Blood for Oil," a slogan that hinted at (but was never given media space to develop) a critique of the political economy that dictates interest in the Middle East in the first place.

In many ways, this concern with the memory of the Vietnam War is at odds with a recurring theme in contemporary political discourse. On several occasions since the late 1970s, the persistence of memory, the public insistence on waving the bloody shirt in the face of promilitary politicians and political pundits, has been proclaimed dead—or lobotomized—with the rise and fall of every new crisis in foreign policy. Interestingly enough, the first widespread emergence of post–Vietnam syndrome jingoism was generated by events in Iran—the hostage crisis of 1979. Such jingoism, coupled with a refurbished politics of spectacle, became a stock-in-trade of the Reagan administration, responsible for the loss of 240 marines in Beirut, the bombing of Libya, and the invasion of Grenada, and of the Bush administration, beginning with the invasion of Panama. All of those minimobilizations of public sentiment, not to mention censorship of news production, now appear in retrospect to have been practice runs, in effect if not in intent, for the destruction of Iraq, which had been militarily reconstructed in the first place because of the Iranian hostage crisis. The war against Iraq to "liberate Kuwait," then, although sold under the sign of a "new world order," was also a war to establish a post–Vietnam syndrome order.

The reason for rehearsing this little story about the persistence of memory and postmodernism's rewriting of the cultural texts of the post-Vietnam hegemony is to suggest that it is possible to identify a recognizable history in it (in the old sense of causality, with one thing more or less leading to another)—a history that, for all the qualitative cultural changes and shifts in theoretical style, represents something more politically compelling than that offered by postmodernist assumptions of absolute breaks and ruptures. For within the popular texts of culture, the opportunity for this kind of organization and management of national sentiment is always a distinct and plausible possibility.

Against the backdrop of the postmodern, a new genre of cultural studies has emerged that is positively affirmative in its embrace of the production and consumption of popular cultural texts. That embrace has come to involve a formula for "doing" cultural studies that claims to draw upon the critical paradigm I outlined in chapter 2, but that nevertheless elides the grittier realities of class and culture that made British culturalism so compelling and so challenging to the status quo in its initial formulations. Meaghan Morris has dubbed this recent development "banal pop-theory," and describes its methodology something like this: "people in modern mediatized societies are complex and contradictory, therefore mass cultural texts are complex and contradictory, therefore people using them produce complex and contradictory culture." Morris speculates that there must be a master disk somewhere "from which thousands of versions of the same article about pleasure, resistance, and the politics of consumption are being run off under different names with minor variations."[17] Usually, that formula dictates that one of a dozen or so assumed others (those who have been critical of mass culture and its patrons) must first be seen off and silenced—the Frankfurt school most often qualifies for the position, but the New York intellectuals, or *Partisan Review* anti-Stalinists, or even the Birmingham school, for example, can be substituted.

This turn to "vox pop" investigations of playful surfaces, and to close readings of cultural texts for their moments of redemptive transgression, perhaps represents a pleasurable and productive activity for academics, but nevertheless it remains politically evasive and ultimately self-defeating unless an effort is made to connect parts to wholes. In refusing any form of determination and totality, some postmodernists forfeit any political sense of the Vietnam era and, at the same time, abandon history to neoconservative revisionists. The attempt to make connections, on the other hand, may help to remind us that terrorizing events, such as wars, scar human bodies in ways that cannot be fully understood in terms of an always already-textualized reality. Moreover, popular cultural texts are not simply and always about spectatorial pleasure and resistance; they also have effects beyond the decoding practices of subscribers and theoreticians. The discursive recycling of Vietnam War representations in books, film, and television, as I have attempted to show, can certainly be thought of in terms of a contestation of meanings. But what cannot be lost sight of is that those texts also conventionalize and make safe more deadly kinds of contestation, where people are not simply silenced or marginalized but are imprisoned, tortured, and killed. Vietnam may well represent a tangle of contradictory discourses, but those discourses still connect to another, not-so-secret history that continues to reverberate in the present.

Representations of the Vietnam War have now become so pervasive, have come to permeate so much of what we consume in the way of words and images in contemporary society, that even those of us who study such things are sometimes hard put to remember precisely what is being rewritten in the process. One of the results of that rewriting has been a sense of guilt over the treatment of America's Vietnam veterans—not guilt over the war itself, the two million dead Vietnamese, the ten million refugees, the destablization of the entire region, the continuing deaths from defoliant toxins that also make large tracks of once-viable farm uninhabitable, but guilt generated by the ongoing classical narrative of the individual victim. That sensibility is now so deeply embedded that it actually became a loudly articulated political tenet of the anti–Gulf War movement, which was at times indistinguishable from prowar groups in proclaiming support for the troops.

The basis for that guilt stems from a persistent theme in the mass cultural retelling of the Vietnam War era that has apparently gained wide acceptance. That is, upon their return Vietnam veterans were silenced, shunned, spit upon by their peers, and made to feel responsible for a war over which they had no control. *Tour of Duty* and *China Beach*, for example, played regularly with that theme, which is the founding principle of the Rambo mystique. But is it true that "the people" silenced the veterans and blamed them for the war? While I would not want to deny the fact of generational conflicts over the war, it is nevertheless true that most veterans returned to their families and communities and got on with their lives as best they could. *Born on the Fourth of July*, both memoir and film, stands as a testament to that fact. When Ron Kovic returned from Vietnam paralyzed from the chest down, his family and friends did what they could for him. That their efforts were ultimately overwhelmed, as was Kovic himself, by more powerful historical forces does not detract from the attempts by family and community to welcome Kovic home. The point is that "the people" did not refuse the veterans ticker tape parades, heroic films, television spectaculars, a decent G.I. bill, responsible veterans hospitals and the like, because "the people" as such do not have access to or control over the kinds of expertise, political decision making, or capital that can arrange and effect such things.

As the Persian Gulf War demonstrated, the power of the media to silence opposition and to drum up mass sentiment on the basis of an assumed mass desire has not diminished. If anything, the power to organize and rearrange domestic space in line with official national policy has increased since the days of the Vietnam War. As one observer of the Persian Gulf War put the case, "we didn't learn to end war with Vietnam, we learned how to manage it."[18] In one of those typical acts of media ventriloquism that Stuart Hall finds so menacing, an episode of the television series *thirtysomething* was built around a cynical version of just that kind of sentiment. "We don't sell war," croons one of the characters, "we simply use war to sell things." But that brief illumination of the advertising industry's ability to yoke together an aesthetic of war with the commodity fetish is quickly lost sight of and dispersed across the melodramatic displacements of the program's competing plot themes. And what is obscured in the process is that war also sells the possibilities for more war.

That war breeds more war is an old tale, of course, and in this book I have attempted to describe some aspects of its retelling. I have also strived to maintain the idea that mass media and war are not exactly the same thing, Paul Virilio's claims notwithstanding, while insisting on the crucial and dialectical relationships among modern subjectivities, war, and mass culture. Long before the first shot is fired and the first body falls, a culture must have in place the discursive means for making such actions possible. The texts of popular culture are one of the sites where this kind of business gets transacted. The Vietnam War generation grew up on the movie and TV images of war in a cultural context structured by the ideological fundamentalism of the Cold War. With significant differences, but creating in the end distressingly similar effects, the present generation has grown up on the Vietnam War in a cultural context of decline and self-interested cynicism. The domestic versions of the Vietnam War (American culture constituting the more crucial battleground), were, and are, waged in terms of a war of representations—a war that will not let us forget that words and images can also wound and kill.

NOTES

Introduction

1. Herr, *Dispatches*, 233.

2. I borrow this formulation from Catherine Clement, who writes, "Somewhere every culture has an imaginary zone for what it excludes, and it is that zone we must try to remember today" (Hélène Cixous and Catherine Clement, *The Newly Born Woman*, tr. Betsy Wing [Minneapolis: University of Minnesota Press, 1986], 6.

3. Jameson, "Reification and Utopia in Mass Culture," 139.

4. Capps, *The Unfinished War*, 147.

5. For discussions of Vietnam War representations in film and television, see Dittmar and Michaud, *From Hanoi to Hollywood*; MacDonald, *Television and the Red Menace*; Wood, *Hollywood from Vietnam to Reagan*; and Auster and Quart, *How the War Was Remembered*. Among surveys of Vietnam War literature, especially useful are Lomperis, *Reading the Wind*; Thomas Myers, *Walking Point: American Narratives of the Vietnam War* (New York: Oxford University Press, 1988); and Jason, *Fourteen Landing Zones*.

6. See also Beidler's second study of Vietnam War literature, *Re-Writing America: Vietnam Authors in Their Generation*.

Chapter 1. The Vietnam Continuum

1. Foucault, *The Archaeology of Knowledge*, 23.

2. For a representative example of the journalism that surrounded Bush's remarks, see *Newsweek*, 10 December 1990. The front cover of this particular issue represents an intense distillation of the political culture that emerged during the buildup to the Gulf War. Set against a black cover, large white lettering proclaims the president's words: "This Will Not Be Another Vietnam." Below the lettering is a relatively small photograph of Bush with fists clenched, meant to portray a sense of steely determination. On either side of the photograph, in smaller white lettering, are two subheadlines: "A Deadline for Democracy" and "A Plan for All-Out War." The former is clearly propagandistic because, even in the wildest of patriotic gestures, the war for the kingdom of Kuwait (at that point still forming in the kingdom of Saudi Arabia) against the military dictatorship in Iraq could hardly be constructed as a war for democracy. The latter headline is a continuation of the main headline in that it promises "all-out war" as opposed to what is, in fact, the myth of half-hearted war in Vietnam. Inside this issue the lead article offers a variation on the dominant media theme of the moment, "the Gulf and the legacy of Vietnam," providing comparisons of a photograph of three soldiers in Saudi Arabia, relaxed and reading a newspaper, with John Olson's famous photograph of the wounded being evacuated from the battle of Hue in 1968.

160

3. See Klare, "Curing the Vietnam Syndrome." Klare has expanded on this article in his book *Beyond the Vietnam Syndrome.*

4. Rowe, "Bringing It All Back Home," p. 197.

5. Pecheux, *Language, Semantics and Ideology,* 111–12, 152–54.

6. Dave Morley, "Texts, Readers, Subjects," in *Culture, Media, Language,* ed. Hall et al., 163–65. I will attempt to show later in this study that subjectivities and even human bodies are malleable entities, as much in flux with history as the cultural and ideological systems that try continually to colonize them.

7. Stephanson, "Interview with Cornel West."

8. The terms *sanitized* and *romanticized* are borrowed from Paul Fussell's preface to *Wartime.*

9. Ross, *No Respect,* 7. Ross's approach to postmodernism is, like that of Cornel West, an exemplary one, refusing as he does to "accept, at face value, the delirious claim of postmodernism to have transcended the problem of elitism or paternalism."

10. MacDonald, *Television and the Red Menace.*

11. Marin, "Coming to Terms with Vietnam," 41, 42–43.

12. Collins, *Uncommon Cultures,* 6.

13. Fussell, *Wartime,* 268, 280.

14. Said, *The World, the Text, and the Critic,* 45. Said goes on to note, borrowing from Nietzsche, that "texts are fundamentally facts of power, not of democratic exchange."

15. Herr, *Dispatches,* 105.

16. Graham Greene, *The Quiet American,* 32, 62, 163.

17. William Lederer and Eugene Burdick, *The Ugly American* (New York: Norton, 1958).

18. According to John Hellmann, in *American Myth and the Legacy of Vietnam, The Ugly American* galvanized President Eisenhower to "order an investigation of the foreign aid program" (17). Hellman insists, moreover, that the book was influential "far beyond its very large readership" and that it helped create the atmosphere in which President Kennedy would call for a national physical-fitness program, declare America's willingness to 'bear any burden,' found the Peace Corps, build up the American Special Forces, and emphasize new tactics of counterinsurgency to combat a communist 'people's war in South Vietnam" (4).

19. Halberstam, "Afterword," in *One Very Hot Day,* 229.

20. Aileu, *The Living-Room War,* xiii. See also Hammond, *The Image Decade,* probably the most comprehensive study to date of the three networks' coverage of Vietnam.

21. I am drawing my terms in this section from Dan Nimmo and James E. Combs, *Mediated Political Realities* (New York: Longman, 1983), 28–33. I also refer to Hammond, *The Image Decade.*

22. Hellmann, *American Myth,* x.

23. R. Williams, *Politics and Letters,* 159.

24. Both of these figures are drawn from Herring, *American's Longest War,* 148, 161.

25. Quoted in Sheehan, *A Bright Shining Lie,* 685.

26. Carl Oglesby, president of Students for a Democratic Society (SDS), quoted in Kendrick, *The Wound Within,* 9.

Chapter 2. Conformity, Consensus, and Cultural Studies

1. Hall, "Notes on Deconstructing the Popular," 235.

2. Ross, *No Respect,* 16.

3. The *New Reasoner* was founded by disillusioned Socialists who, in the wake of the Soviet invasion of Hungary in 1956, sought to reinstate the more philosophical,

international, and humane aspects of the Marxist tradition against the Stalinist authoritarian model that had come to dominate the Soviet Union. Unlike many of their intellectual counterparts in the United States, however, this act of rethinking was not predicated on a wholesale retreat into the reactionary cultural politics of the Cold War. At about the same time, the *Universities and Left Review* was founded, again by dissident Socialists, but this journal was more concerned with issues of popular culture and the emerging postwar systems of consumer culture that were beginning to enter political debate. Both groups overlapped somewhat and eventually, through the mass demonstrations organized by the Campaign for Nuclear Disarmament, would come together to form the *New Left Review.* This New Left would also be instrumental in the formation of the Vietnam Solidarity Campaign. For a discussion of this history from the point of view of someone who was at its center, see R. Williams, *Politics and Letters*, 361–72. Perhaps the best example of American intellectual attitudes in this same period is to be found in the special issue of *Partisan Review,* "Our Country and Our Culture," 19 (1952), and in the collection of essays to be found in *Mass Culture: The Popular Arts in America*, ed. Bernard Rosenberg and David Manning White (New York: Free Press, 1957).

4. See Kerber, "Diversity and the Transformation of American Studies." Kerber praises the diversity of American studies in the 1950s, but points out that a decidedly "cold war agenda" permeated the American studies movement. The curriculum, as she encountered it in the 1950s, "involved the strident validation of American exceptionalism." The resulting intellectual direction of the movement was thus drained "of political content or political responsibility" (419).

5. Tate, *The Search for a Method in American Studies*, 6

6. Tremaine McDowell, *American Studies*, 33.

7. Huber, "A Theory of American Studies," 268.

8. Pearce, "American Studies as a Discipline," 181.

9. Ibid., 183.

10. The study of myth as collective representation comes from H. Smith, *Virgin Land*, xi. See Tate's *Search* for a more detailed account of the myth symbolist's approach to literature. For a sharply critical assessment of myth symbolism, see Kuklick, "Myth and Symbol in American Studies."

11. H. Smith, "Can American Studies Develop a Method?," 14–15.

12. F. O. Matthessen, *American Renaissance: Art and Expression in the Age of Emerson and Whitman* (New York: Oxford University Press, 1941). The renaissance canon set forth by Matthessen has been critically reexamined by some of the younger generation of Americanists. In particular see Michaels and Pease. eds., *The American Renaissance Reconsidered*, a collection of essays that questions the various overt and covert aspects of Matthessen's project. Specifically, see Jane Thompkins, "The Other American Renaissance" (34–57), which restores the wider literary and cultural world otherwise suppressed by Matthessen's selection, and Donald Pease, "Moby Dick and the Cold War" (113–55), which suggests that the supression of alternative literary voices in *American Renaissance* was due to Cold War political demands on intellectuals to produce work within the ideological paradigm of consensus. Thus Matthessen eliminated both his own dissenting political tendencies and those of mid-nineteenth-century America.

13. Myra Jehlen, "Introduction: Beyond Transcendence," in *Ideology and Classic American Literature*, ed. Bercovitch and Jehlen, 3.

14. In his introduction to the anthology *American Studies*, Robert Merideth writes that it is not an "impossible exaggeration" to say that since the publication of Kroeber and Kluckhohn's study, "all significant theoretical discussion in the social sciences has revolved around some aspect" of the culture concept (x). On this point, see also Mechling et al., "American Cultural Studies," 363–89.

15. Walker, *American Studies in the United States*, 59–60.

16. Kroeber and Kluckhohn, *Culture*, p 181.

17. Richard E. Sykes, "American Studies and the Concept of Culture," 254.

18. Ibid., 256. On this point, see also Katz, "Culture and Literature in American Studies," in which Katz is critical of the inadequacies of Sykes's borrowed culture theory and suggests instead the theory of Leslie White as a more likely source for explaining the cultural role of literature.

19. This overview of the transitions in Kroeber's work, and of the influence of Parsons and Kluckhohn, is distilled from Harris, *Cultural Materialism*, esp. 278–80.

20. Kroeber and Kluckhohn, *Culture*, p. 181.

21. Quoted in Harris, *Cultural Materialism*, 280.

22. For the classic statement of the view, see Bell, *The End of Ideology*. See also Talcott Parsons, *The Social System* (New York: Free Press, 1951).

23. For a critical review of structural functionalism, see Harris, *Cultural Materialism*. An extremely useful collection of essay that criticize the notion of pluralism is Gurevitch et al., eds., *Culture, Society, and the Media*.

24. Stuart Hall, "The Rediscovery of Ideology: Return of the Repressed in Media Studies," in *Culture, Society, and the Media*, ed. Gurevitch et al., 59–60.

25. Leo Marx, "Thoughts on the Origins and Character of the American Studies Movement," 400. Robert F. Berkhofer, Jr., writing in the same issue of *American Quarterly*, makes a similar point concerning the Cold War roots of American studies in his essay "The Americanness of American Studies" (340–45). See also Sklar, "The Problems of an American Studies Philosophy," which makes the point that the poverty of theory in American studies is due in part to the "reluctance" to engage with the "Marxist intellectual tradition." Sklar suggests that this reluctance stems from the "legacy of the Cold War and the links between American Studies and United States foreign policy objectives."

26. Hall, "The Rediscovery of Ideology," 61.

27. Wise, "Paradigm Dramas in American Studies," 311–12.

28. This did not mean that myth symbolism simply disappeared, or that liberal humanist literary criticism no longer played a role in American studies. Indeed, the humanists could still mount a spirited counterattack. See, for example, Marx, "American Studies," in which Marx looks back across the years from 1969 to Smith's 1957 essay and sees no reason to revise Smith's central tenets. However, Kuklick's 1972 critique of the unquestioned humanist assumptions of myth symbolism, like Tate's 1973 demolition of the myth symbolists' ethnocentric notion of holism, is a good indication of the gap that had opened up between the generation of the 1950s and that of the 1960s.

29. See in particular Kolodny, *The Lay of the Land*.

30. Slotkin, *The Fatal Environment*, xi. See also his earlier study of the frontier, *Regeneration through Violence*, which argues that frontier mythology works to hide what was, in reality, a deeply imperialistic process of American development.

31. Eagleton, *The Function of Criticism*, 85–86.

32. Wise, "Paradigm Dramas," 314.

33. Ibid.

34. Even the Modern Language Association was driven toward social and political criticism in these years, passing resolutions that opposed the Vietnam War and the draft. In 1971 Louis Kampf, a vehement and outspoken opponent to the war and an active member of SDS and Resist, was elected president of the MLA. In that same year the Commission on the Status of Women in the Profession was proposed. On these issues see Leitch, *American Literary Criticism*, 371–79.

35. Marx, "Thoughts," 400–401.

36. Kelly, "Literature and the Historian," 143. I am making use of Kelly's essay because it attempts to go beyond merely criticizing myth symbolism to suggest an alternative method of approaching literature in culture, and because the specific anthropological and sociological theories from which Kelly builds his argument

were central to the development of American studies during the 1970s and 1980s. Moreover, such borrowings demonstrate the continuing refusal to grapple with the most basic texts of critical cultural studies, especially those that stem from within the Marxist tradition. In particular, there has been a noticeable reluctance to deal with concepts of ideology and the practices of political power in culture.

37. Ibid., 147.

38. Anthony F. C. Wallace, *Culture and Personality* (New York: Random House, 1970), 22–24.

39. Kelly, "Literature and the Historian," 148.

40. Ibid., 152.

41. Berger and Luckmann, *The Social Construction of Reality,* 47–48.

42. Kelly, "Literature and the Historian," 153. For another attempt within American studies to synthesize the phenomenology of Berger and Luckmann with Wallace's cognitive, personality, and cultural approach, see Jay Mechling, "In Search of an American Ethnoscience," in *The Study of American Culture,* ed. Luedtke, 241–77.

43. Geertz, *The Interpretation of Culture,* 5–11. Geertz defines his "concept of culture" as "essentially a semiotic one. Believing with Weber that man is an animal suspended in webs of significance he himself has spun, I take culture to be those webs, and the analysis of it to be therefore not an experimental science in search of a law but an interpretative one in search of meaning. It is explication I am after, construing social expressions upon their surface enigmatical" (5).

44. For a critique of the delimited approach to ideology taken by Berger and Luckmann and by Geertz, see Robert Wuthnow et al., eds., *Cultural Analysis: The Work of Berger, Douglas, Foucault, and Habermas* (London: Routledge and Kegan Paul, 1984). In particular, see Cecil Tate's study "The Critical Theory of Jürgen Habermas" (179–239), a good example of the muddled thinking thay has developed around the concept of ideology in American studies. Tate's *Search for a Method* is especially illuminating in its consistent attempt to separate ideology from every category of communication, whether communication is taken to be symbolic, mythic, or linguistic (see esp. 20–22, 66–68, 81–82).

45. Hall, "The Rediscovery of Ideology," 65–66. Although I am borrowing the idea of "critical paradigm" from Hall, this is in no way meant to suggest that what follows is precisely what he had in mind when he coined the term.

46. For a useful overview of the influence of Williams, as well as of E. P. Thompson and Richard Hoggart, and the subsequent development of cultural studies, see Stuart Hall, "Cultural Studies at the Centre: Some Problematics and Problems," in *Culture, Media, Language,* ed. Hall et al. Although Hall is talking specifically about the developments at the Centre for Contemporary Cultural Studies at the University of Birmingham, in terms of the general evolution of cultural studies his remarks remain extremely pertinent. The immense influence of these scholars on developments in cultural and historical studies in the United States is attested to in the footnotes and indexes of numerous articles and books. For a sustained discussion of this influence, see the special issue "Marxism and History: The British Contribution," *Radical Historical Review* 19 (Winter 1978–79).

47. An interesting discussion of the influence of Williams's work on younger intellectuals can be found in Martin and Petro, "An Interview With Terry Eagleton." Talking about the situation in the late 1960s and 1970s, Eagleton says that many younger leftist-intellectuals "moved into what we took to be a more rigorous and in some ways more politically relevant form of theory and, from that perspective, it looked as though Williams was standing still. . . . But it is dangerous to think you have preempted, or got beyond Williams because he has the curious knack . . . of actually holding a position . . . that you end up endorsing." Eagleton goes on to say that in his work and political activities Williams was prefiguring "the kinds of positions and forms of allegiance that people now find themselves with [in] his attitude

towards the critic's role in the academy, his attitude about what literary criticism should be, and even his stance toward cultural studies and the need to transgress interdisciplinary boundaries" (85–86).

48. R. Williams, *Marxism and Literature*, 11.

49. Ibid.

50. Raymond Williams, *The Sociology of Culture* (New York: Schocken Books, 1982), 10.

51. For an analysis of this use of the culture concept, see R. Williams, *Culture and Society, 1780–1950*. Williams also traces Arnold's position as it developed in opposition to the emerging industrial social formation, and the social unrest that accompanied it, in *Problems in Materialism and Culture*, 3–8. For a more Americanist approach to these questions, particularly as they can be found in the writings of Tylor, Arnold, and Walt Whitman, see Alan Trachtenberg, "American Studies as a Cultural Program," in *Ideology and Classic American Literature*, ed. Bercovitch and Jehlen, 172–87.

52. Raymond Williams, *The Long Revolution* (Harmondsworth, England: Penguin Books, 1961), 61–62. Although the model of culture as a whole way of life might at first glance seem to run parallel to such myth symbolist notions as "organic unity," "functional interrelationships," and "conformity of values," it should be noted that Williams is not working within the structural functionalist, consensus paradigm that was so influential in the American academy during the 1950s and 1960s. In fact, Williams insists that culture must be understood as whole way of life and struggle. Conflict, not consensus, stands at the center of Williams's Marxist model of cultural formation.

53. R. Williams, *Problems*, 20.

54. Gunn, *The Culture of Criticism and the Criticism of Culture*, 166.

55. Gramsci's approach to questions of culture and hegemony can be found in *Selections from the Prison Notebooks*, trans Quintin Hoare and Geoffrey Nowell Smith, and *Selections from Cultural Writings*, trans. William Boelhower (Cambridge: Harvard University Press, 1985). For a demonstration of how Gramsci's theories might be deployed in areas of interest to American studies, see Denning, *Mechanic Accents*, and Todd Gitlin, "Television's Screens: Hegemony in Transition," in *American Media and Mass Culture*, ed. Lazere, 240–65.

56. R. Williams, *Problems*, 34.

57. Belsey, *Critical Practice*, 5.

58. Althusser, *Lenin and Philosophy*, 158–61

59. See Louis Althusser, *For Marx*, trans. Ben Brewster (London: Allen Lane, 1969) and *Lenin and Philosophy*, esp. "Ideology and Ideological State Apparatuses," 127–86. For a critique of Althusser's position, see Lovell, *Pictures of Reality*, and, more recently, Collins, *Uncommon Cultures*. The main complaint leveled against Althusser is that his theory leaves no room for political struggle or conflict. Every form of human activity, accordingly, is locked into dominant ideology.

60. On this point, see de Lauretis, *Alice Doesn't*.

61. Said, *The World, The Text, and The Critic*, 176.

62. Hall, "Notes on Deconstructing the Popular."

63. Gramsci, *Prison Notebooks*, 210.

64. Hall et al., *Policing the Crisis*, 217.

65. R. Williams, *Marxism and Literature*, 121–27.

66. Hall, "Notes," 237.

67. See, for example, Rowe, "Bringing It All Back Home," and Berman, "Rambo."

68. Marx, "Thoughts," 401.

Chapter 3. Writing the War

1. Schlesinger, *The Bitter Heritage*, *31–32*. Although Schlesinger did not invent the term *quagmire thesis* (the term *quagmire* as applied to Vietnam was first introduced

into the American political lexicon in 1964 by David Halberstam in *The Making of a Quagmire*), he was one of the first "insiders" to use it at length as an explanation of how the United States became involved in Vietnam.

2. Karnow, *Vietnam*, 11.

3. The latest repetition of this part of the paradigm (that I am aware of, at least) can be found in Perret, *A Country Made by War*, 537.

4. Apart from Schlesinger, *Bitter Heritage*, see Richard Goodwin, *Triumph or Tragedy* and *Remembering America*. See also Hoopes, *The Limits of Intervention*, and Chester Cooper, *Lost Crusade*.

5. Two studies that deal with this emergent concern, and that were widely read at the time of their publication, are Theodore Roszak, *The Making of a Counter Culture*, and Reich, *The Greening of America*.

6. Schlissel, ed., *The World of Randolph Bourne*, 198–99. See also Christopher Lasch's study of Bourne's career and influence in *The New Radicalism in America*.

7. Quoted in Ungar, *The Movement*, 25.

8. For a cogent discussion of liberal pluralism and the Cold War see Ross, *No Respect*, esp. chapter 2, "Containing Culture in the Cold War."

9. Schlissel, ed., *The World of Randolph Bourne*, 199.

10. Benda, *The Treason of the Intellectuals*.

11. Fridjonsdottir, "The Modern Intellectual," 116.

12. Gouldner, *The Future of Intellectuals and the Rise of the New Class*, 1.

13. Fridjonsdottir, "The Modern Intellectual," 111.

14. See Halberstam, *The Best and the Brightest*.

15. Ladd and Lipsett, *Academics, Politics, and the 1972 Election*, 1.

16. Alexander Bloom, *Prodigal Sons*, 347, 341.

17. See Krupnick, *Lionel Trilling and the Fate of Cultural Criticism*, esp. chapter 8, "The Fate of Modernism."

18. Gramsci, *Prison Notebooks*, 5.

19. Quoted in Bloom, *Prodigal Sons*, 324.

20. Chomsky, *American Power and the New Mandarins* 310.

21. For an account of the friendship between Ellsberg and Vann, see Sheehan, *A Bright Shining Lie*, 593–98.

22. See Ellsberg, *Papers on the War*. It will be remembered that following leaks to the press concerning the secret bombing of Cambodia in 1969, President Nixon created the clandestine internal security unit called the "Plumbers." The Plumbers were also responsible for breaking into the office of Ellsberg's psychiatrist, where they hoped to find damaging personal information.

23. Ibid., 1.

24. Steel, *Walter Lippmann and the American Century*, 541–42.

25. Quoted in ibid., 558.

26. Quoted in ibid., 557.

27. MacLeish quoted in Goldman, *The Tragedy of Lyndon Johnson*, 510.

28. Quoted in ibid., pp. 510–11.

29. Quoted in Vogelgesang, *The Long Dark Night of the Soul*, 65.

30. Quoted in Goldman, *Tragedy*, 505–6.

31. The telegram—written by Robert Silvers, editor of the *New York Review of Books*, and the poet Stanley J. Kunitz—read in part: "We would like you to know that others of us share his [Lowell's] dismay at recent American foreign policy decisions. . . . We hope that people in this and other countries will not conclude that a White House arts program testifies to approval of Administration policy by the members of the artistic community." (quoted in Vogelgesang, *Long Dark Night*, 196).

32. Quoted in Goldman, *Tragedy*, 533.

33. An indication of the distance between the intellectual community and the government by the early 1970s can be found in a speech given by Vice President

Spiro Agnew: "The last decade saw the most precipitous decline in respect for law and order in our history. Some of those who call each other 'intellectuals' helped to sow the wind, and America reaped the whirlwind" (quoted in Vogelgesang, *Long Dark Night*, 158). Of course, the intellectuals could point to Agnew himself as an indication of how far the government had moved from intellectual discourse.

34. A selection of books on the New Left would include Disch and Schwartz, eds., *Hard Rains*, Stolz, ed., *The Politics of the New Left*; and Ungar, *The Movement*.

35. Clausewitz, *On War*.

36. See Sloterdijk, *Critique of Cynical Reasoning*.

37. Marin, "Coming to Terms with Vietnam." 41–56.

38. Halberstam, *One Very Hot Day*, 299. Page references, hereafter in the text, are taken from the Warner Books reprint.

39. A number of novels and memoirs (the distinction is never concrete in Vietnam War literature) that were published in the late 1960s and early 1970s went out of print fairly quickly. In the present period of renewed interest in Vietnam, some of these have been reissued. See, for example, Bunting, *The Lionheads*; Crumley, *One To Count Cadence*; Davis, *Coming Home*; Eastlake, *The Bamboo Bed*; Huggett, *Body Count*; Tim O'Brien, *If I Should Die in a Combat Zone* (New York: Reed, 1969; reprint 1980); Pelfrey, *The Big V*; Sloan, *War Games*; and J. Williams, *Captain Blackman*.

40. Lomperis, *Reading the Wind*, 41.

41. Quoted in ibid.

42. Quoted in ibid.

43. Zalin Grant, "Vietnam as Fable," 23.

44. Ibid.

45. Kovic, *Born on the Fourth of July*, 74. Page references, hereafter in the text, are to the Pocket Books reprint.

46. Caputo, *A Rumor of War*, 128. Page references, hereafter in the text, are to the Ballantine reprint.

47. Herr, *Dispatches*, 267. Page references, hereafter in the text, are to the Avon Books reprint.

48. O'Brien, *Going after Cacciato*. Page references, hereafter in the text, are to the Dell reprint.

49. Kazin, "Vietnam," 120–21.

50. Webb, *Fields of Fire*, 56,

51. Gitlin, *Inside Primetime*, 227.

52. *The Washington Post* (July 12, 1980) p.8.

53. Caputo, *A Rumor of War*, 317.

54. Mason, *In Country*, 79; hereafter cited in the text.

Chapter 4. Vietnam in Hollywood

1. Fussell, *Wartime*, 268–70. Fussell's reference to *South Pacific* is quoted from John Ellis, *The Sharp End of War* (1980).

2. *Time*, 26 Jan. 1987, 3.

3. David Halberstam, review of *Platoon*, *New York Times*, 8 March 1987, 21, 38.

4. See, for example, J. Smith, *Looking Away*. Lawrence Suid makes a similar point in *Guts and Glory*.

5. Roth, "Some Warners Musicals and the Spirit of the New Deal."

6. One of the best-known attempts to analyze the Western in this way is Wright, *Sixguns and Society*. See also Philip French, *Westerns: Aspects of a Movie Genre* (New York: Viking Press, 1973).

7. Jameson, "Reification and Utopia in Mass Culture," 141.

8. Ibid., 142. Here Jameson is analyzing *Jaws* (1975), and in particular the symbolic and ideological role of the killer shark, a reading that I have borrowed because it

runs so close to popular filmic representations of the threat posed by the Vietnamese guerilla fighter.

9. Trachtenberg, *The Incorporation of America*, 28.

10. Gilman, *Difference and Pathology*, 239.

11. Virilio, *War and Cinema*, 1.

12. Ibid., 8.

13. Sontag, "The Imagination of Disaster," 42.

14. For a more complete overview of these films, see Adair, *Vietnam on Film*.

15. Brewin, "TV's Newest Villain"; Heilbronn, "Coming Home a Hero."

16. See Slotkin, "Gunfighters and Green Berets," which argues that many of the Westerns of the 1960s, particularly those set in Mexico, were indirect articulations of the cultural crisis set in motion by the war in Vietnam. *The Magnificent Seven* (1960), on the other hand, emerged out of a pre-1960s ethos when the "mystique" of counterinsurgency was still operating at the level of a romantic imaginary.

17. See, for example, Murray, "Hollywood, Nihilism, and the Youth Culture of the Sixties."

18. For an overview of rock music's relationship to the politics of protest in the late 1960s, see Marcus, *Mystery Train*. See also Denisoff and Peterson, eds., *The Sounds of Social Change*.

19. See Adair, *Vietnam on Film*, and McCarthy and Flynn, eds., *King of the B's*. For a more recent working-over of the ideological themes in the films of the 1960s, see the first chapter of Ryan and Kellner, *Camera Politica*.

20. For a discussion of the historical significance of *The Green Berets* in relation to the myths of the 1960s, see Spark, "The Soldier at the Heart of the War."

21. On this point, see Suid, *Guts and Glory*, 228.

22. Ibid., 222.

23. Ibid., 221.

24. For a useful discussion of the Pentagon's attempt to influence the content of war films, see Lawrence Suid, "Hollywood and Vietnam," *Film Comment*, 15 (September-October 1979): 20–25.

25. Quoted in Suid, *Guts and Glory*, 233.

26. Quart and Auster, *American Film and Society since 1945*, 90.

27. *Hollywood Reporter*, 17 July 1968, 3.

28. Dickstein, *Gates of Eden*; 271.

29. Recent studies that assume these metaphors as a structuring principle include Capps, *The Unfinished War*; Wheeler, *Touched with Fire*; MacPherson, *Long Time Passing*; Loren Baritz, *Backfire*; and Scruggs and Swerdlow, *To Heal a Nation*.

30. Hayden, *Reunion*, 434–35. According to Hayden, Kovic became "the model for the character played by Jon Voight in *Coming Home*." (435), a film that Jane Fonda helped to proiduce and in which she starred. See also the interview with Jane Fonda and Tom Hayden in *Rolling Stone*, 5 November–10 December 1987, 123–28.

31. Philip French's review of *The Deer Hunter* in the London *Observer*, 4 March 1979, quoted in Kauffmann, "The Hunting of the Hunters."

32. Two of the most thoroughly argued studies of the sexual nature of Mike and Nick's relationship are to be found in Wood, *Hollywood from Vietnam to Reagan*, and Jeffords, *The Remasculinization of America*.

33. Sontag, "Fascinating Fascism." See also Dempsey, "Hellbent for Mystery." On the development of a fascist aesthetic in 1980s films about the Vietnam War, see Hoberman, "The Fascist Guns in the West."

34. The literary roots of the masculine codes of hunting and war that can be said to inform *The Deer Hunter* can be traced to the modern period, specifically to the writings of Faulkner, Hemingway, and Mailer. See Marsha Kinder, "Political Game"; see also David Axeen, "Eastern Western," *Film Quarterly* 32, no. 4 (Summer 1979): 17–18.

35. Wood, *Hollywood from Vietnam to Reagan*.

36. Conrad, *Heart of Darkness*, 101; hereafter cited in the text.

37. Wood, *Hollywood From Vietnam to Reagan*, 46–49, 50, 30.

38. Ibid., 69.

39. For a more detailed discussion of the Asner case, see Gitlin, *Inside Prime Time*, 10.

40. See *Variety*, 9 February 1982, 1, 19.

41. See *Variety*, 19 November 1981, 1. For a thorough investigation of the personalities behind the blacklisting, see Ceplair and Englund, *The Inquisition in Hollywood*.

42. See Gitlin, *Inside Prime Time*, 3–12.

43. *Variety*, 22 February 1982, 1, 20.

44. C. Smith, "The Rehabilitation of the U.S. Military in Films since 1978."

45. Sarris, "The Screen at the End of the Tunnel."

46. Berman, "Rambo."

47. *Platoon* is semiautobiographical, based as it is to a large extent on Oliver Stone's personal experiences as a soldier in Vietnam. In many ways, writing the film script was a cathartic act on Stone's part, an attempt to lay the ghosts of his own Vietnam experience and to help him through the difficult period of readjustment following his return to the United States. In fact, Stone had been trying for ten years to get Hollywood studios interested in his manuscript of *Platoon*. Eventually a British company, Hemdale, advanced Stone the necessary financing to get the project off the ground.

48. *Time*, 26 Jan. 1987, 54–61.

49. David Halberstam, review of *Platoon*, *New York Times*, 8 March 1987, 21.

50. Cawley, "An Ex-Marine Sees *Platoon*," 7.

51. MacCabe, "Realism and the Cinema."

52. For what is perhaps the most complete analysis of the World War II combat film see Basinger, *The World War II Combat Film*.

53. Thomas Elsaesser, "Vincent Minnelli," in *Home Is Where the Heart Is*, ed. Gledhill, 222.

Chapter 5. Melodramatic Excess: The Body in/of the Text

1. See O'Hallaren, "It's Back to the Beach for Dana Delany," 10–13.

2. Gallagher and Laqueur, eds., *The Making of the Modern Body*, vii.

3. Foucault, *The History of Sexuality*, 1:141.

4. Foucault, *Discipline and Punish*, 153.

5. Butler, "Variations on Sex and Gender," 131.

6. The United States, of course, is not the only country to have lost a war in the twentieth century or to have suffered disruptions in cultural production and political discourses as a result. Historical studies of Germany during the aftermath of World War I, for example, often focus on psychosexual themes in art, cinema, and politics in order to explain the erratic course of events that swept through the Weimar period. The standard works that investigate Weimar culture in this way are Lotte Eisner, *The Haunted Screen: Expressionism in the German Film and the Influence of Max Reinhardt* (Berkeley and Los Angeles: University of California Press, 1969); Siegfried Kracauer, *From Caligari to Hitler: A Psychological History of German Film* (Princeton, N.J.: Princeton University Press, 1947); and Peter Gay, *Weimar Culture: The Outsider as Insider* (New York: Harper & Row, 1970). These studies have been challenged, and in many ways surpassed, by Patrice Petro's *Joyless Streets: Women and Melodramatic Representation in Weimar Germany* (Princeton, N.J.: Princeton University Press, 1989), and by Theweleit, *Male Fantasies*.

7. Corliss, review of *Platoon*, 56.

8. Auster and Quart, *How the War Was Remembered*; 112–113.

9. Gledhill, ed., *Home Is Where the Heart Is*, 6.

10. Geoffrey Nowell-Smith, "Minnelli and Melodrama," in *Home Is Where the Heart Is*, ed. Gledhill, 70–74.

11. Ibid., 72.

12. Brooks, *The Melodramatic Imagination*, quoted in Christine Gledhill, "The Melodramatic Field: An Investigation," in *Home Is Where the Heart Is*, ed. Gledhill, 31.

13. Gledhill, "The Melodramatic Field," 31.

14. Ibid., 31–32.

15. Jeffords, *The Remasculinization of America*, 146–47.

16. Daniel Ellsberg's description, taken from *Papers on the War*, 1.

17. Morris, "Banality in Cultural Studies," 19, 15.

18. *In These Times* (February 1991) :3.

WORKS CITED

Adair, Gilbert. *Vietnam on Film: From "The Green Berets" to "Apocalypse Now."* New York: Proteus, 1981.

Adler, Renate. "The Absolute End of the Romance of War." *New York Times*, 20 June 1968, 49.

Althusser, Louis. *Lenin and Philosophy and Other Essays.* Translated by Ben Brewster. New York: Monthly Review Press, 1971.

Arlen, Michael. *The Living-Room War.* Harmondsworth: Penguin, 1984.

———. *The View From Highway 1.* New York: Farrar, Straus & Giroux, 1976.

Auster, Arnold, and Leonard Quart. "Hollywood in Vietnam: The Triumph of the Will." *Cineaste* 9 (1979): 4–9.

———. *How the War Was Remembered: Hollywood and Vietnam.* New York: Praeger, 1988.

Baker, Mark. *Nam.* New York: Morrow, 1981.

Baldwin, Neil. "Going After the War." *Publisher's Weekly,* 11 February 1983, 34–38.

Baritz, Loren. *Backfire: American Culture and the Vietnam War.* New York: Ballantine, 1985.

Barnouw, Erik. *Tube of Plenty: The Evolution of American Television.* New York: Oxford University Press, 1975.

Barrett, Michele, et al. *Ideology and Cultural Production.* New York: St. Martin's Press, 1979.

Barthes, Roland. *Mythologies.* London: Paladin, 1973.

Basinger, Jeanine. *The World War II Combat Film: Anatomy of a Genre.* New York: Columbia University Press, 1986.

Baudrillard, Jean. *Simulations.* Translated by Paul Foss, Paul Patton, and Philip Beitchman. New York: Semiotext(e), 1983.

Beidler, Philip. *American Literature and the Experience of Vietnam.* Athens: University of Georgia Press, 1982.

———. *Re-Writing America: Vietnam Veterans in Their Genera-tion.* Athens: University of Georgia Press, 1991.

Bell, Daniel. *The End of Ideology.* New York: Free Press, 1960.

Belsey, Catherine. *Critical Practice.* London: Methuen, 1980.

Benda, Julian. *The Treason of the Intellectuals.* Translated by Richard Aldington. New York: Morrow, 1928.

Benjamin, Walter. "Theories of German Fascism: On the Collection of Essays *War and Warrior,* Edited by Ernst Junger." Translated by Jerolf Wikoff. *New German Critique* 17 (Spring 1979): 120–28.

Bercovitch, Sacvan, and Myra Jehlen, eds. *Ideology and Classic American Literature.* New York: Cambridge University Press, 1986.

Berg, Rick. "Losing Vietnam: Covering the War in an Age of Technology." *Cultural Critique* 3 (Spring 1986): 92–125.

Berger, Peter L., and Thomas Luckmann. *The Social Construction of Reality: A Treatise in the Sociology of Knowledge.* New York: Doubleday, 1967.

Berkhofer, Robert F., Jr. "The Americanness of American Studies." *American Quarterly* 31, no. 3 (Fall 1979): 340–45.

Berman, Russell A. "Rambo: From Counter-Culture to Contra." *Telos* no. 64 (Summer 1985): 143–47.

Bloom, Alexander. *Prodigal Sons: The New York Intellectuals and Their World.* New York: Oxford University Press, 1986.

Boyer, Peter. "Is It Prime Time for Vietnam?" *New York Times,* 2 August 1987, 1, 16.

Bradbury, Malcolm. "The Future of American Studies." In *Other Voices, Other Views,* edited by Rubin Winks, 32–41. Westport, Conn.: Greenwood Press, 1978.

Brenkmann, John. "Mass Media: From Collective Experience to the Culture of Privatization." *Social Text* 1 (Winter 1979): 94–109.

Brewin, Robert. "TV's Newest Villain: The Vietnam Veteran." *TV Guide,* 19 July 1975, 4–8.

Britten, Andrew. "Sideshows: Hollywood in Vietnam." *Movie* nos. 27–28 (Winter-Spring 1980–81): 2–23.

Brooks, Peter. *The Melodramatic Imagination: Balzac, Henry James, Melodrama, and the Mode of Excess.* New Haven, Conn.: Yale University Press, 1976.

Brzezinski, Zbigniew. "Interview." *U.S. News and World Report,* 16 April 1979, 49–50.

Bunting, Josiah. *The Lionheads.* New York: Braziller, 1972.

Butler, Judith. "Variations on Sex and Gender: Beauvoir, Wittig, and Foucault." In *Feminism as Critique,* edited by Seyla Benhabib and Drucilla Cornell, 128–42. Minneapolis: University of Minnesota Press, 1987.

Callenbach, Ernest. "Phallic Nightmare." *Film Quarterly* 32, no. 4 (Summer 1979): 18–22.

Capps, Walter H. *The Unfinished War: Vietnam and the American Consciousness.* Boston: Beacon Press, 1982.

Caputo, Philip. *A Rumor of War.* New York: Random House, 1977. Reprint. New York: Ballantine, 1982.

Cawley, Leo. "An Ex-Marine Sees *Platoon.*" *Monthly Review* 39, no. 2 (June 1987): 6–18.

Ceplair, Larry, and Steven Englund. *The Inquisition in Hollywood: Politics in the Film Community, 1930–1960.* New York: Anchor Books, 1980.

Chomsky, Noam. *American Power and the New Mandarins.* New York: Pantheon Books, 1967.

Clark, Michael. "Remembering Vietnam." *Cultural Critique* 3 (Spring 1986): 46–78.

Clausewitz, Carl von. *On War.* Princeton, N.J.: Princeton University Press, 1976.

Collins, Jim. *Uncommon Cultures: Popular Culture and Post-Modernism.* New York: Routledge, 1989.

Conrad, Joseph. *Heart of Darkness.* Harmondsworth, England: Penguin Books, 1983.

Cooper, Chester. *Lost Crusade: America in Vietnam.* New York: Dodd, Mead, 1970.

Corliss, Richard. Review of *Platoon. Time*, 26 January 1987, 54–61.

Crawford, Alan. *Thunder on the Right: The 'New Right' and the Politics of Resentment.* New York: Pantheon Books, 1980.

Crumley, James. *One to Count Cadence* New York: Random House, 1969.

de Lauretis, Teresa. *Alice Doesn't: Feminism, Semiotics, Cinema.* Bloomington: Indiana University Press, 1984.

Davis, George. *Coming Home.* New York: Random House, 1971.

Dempsey, Michael. "Hellbent for Mystery." *Film Quarterly* 32 no. 4 (Summer 1979): 10–13.

Denisoff, R. Serge, and Richard A. Peterson, eds. *The Sounds of Social Change.* Chicago: Rand McNally, 1972.

Denning, Michael. *Mechanic Accents: Dime Novels and Working-Class Culture in America.* London: Verso, 1987.

Dickstein, Morris. "Bringing It All Back Home." *Partisan Review* 45, no. 4 (1978): 627–33.

———. *Gates of Eden: American Culture in the Sixties.* New York: Basic Books, 1977.

Disch, Robert, and Barry N. Schwartz, eds. *Hard Rains: Conflict and Conscience in America.* New York: Random House, 1970.

Dittmar, Linda, and Gene Michaud. *From Hanoi to Hollywood: The Vietnam War in American Film.* New Brunswick, N.J.: Rutgers University Press, 1990.

Donald, James, and Stuart Hall. *Politics and Ideology.* Milton Keynes: Open University Press, 1986.

Draper, Theodore. "Ghosts of Vietnam." *Dissent* (Winter 1979): 30–42.

Durden, Charles. *No Bugles No Drums.* New York: Avon Books, 1984.

Eagleton, Terry. *Criticism and Ideology: A Study in Marxist Literary Theory.* London: Verso, 1982.

———. *The Function of Criticism: From the Spectator to Post-Structuralism.* London: Verso, 1984.

Eastlake, William. *The Bamboo Bed.* New York: Simon & Schuster, 1969.

Ellsberg, Daniel. *Papers on the War.* New York: Simon & Schuster, 1972.

Emerson, Gloria. "Our Man in Antibes: Graham Greene." *Rolling Stone,* 9 March 1978, 45–49.

———. *Winners and Losers: Battles, Retreats, Gains, Losses, and Ruins from the Vietnam War.* New York: Random House, 1976.

Enzenberger, Hans Magnus. *The Consciousness Industry: On Literature, Politics, and the Media.* New York: Continuum Books, 1974.

Ewen, Stuart, and Elizabeth Ewen. *Channels of Desire: Mass Images and the Shaping of American Consciousness.* New York: McGraw-Hill, 1982.

Eyerman, Ron, Lennart G. Svensson, and Thomas Soderqvist, eds. *Intellectuals, Universities, and the State in Western Modern Societies.* Berkeley and Los Angeles: University of California Press, 1987.

Fitzgerald, Frances. *Fire in the Lake: The Vietnamese and the Americans in Vietnam.* Boston: Little, Brown, 1972.

Fluck, Winfried. "Aesthetic Premises in American Studies." In *Other Voices, Other Views,* edited by Robin Winks, 20–21. Westport, Conn.: Greenwood Press, 1978.

Foucault, Michel. *The Archaeology of Knowledge.* Translated by A. M. Sheridan Smith. New York: Pantheon Books, 1982.

———. *Discipline and Punish: The Birth of the Prison.* Translated by Alan Sheridan. New York: Vintage Books, 1979.

———. *The History of Sexuality,* volume 1. Translated by Robert Hurley. New York: Vintage Books, 1980.

Fridjonsdottir, Katrin. "The Modern Intellectual: In Power or Disarmed?" In *Intellectuals, Universities, and the State in Western*

Modern Societies, edited by Ron Eyerman, Lennart G. Svensson, and Thomas Soderqvist. Berkeley and Los Angeles: University of California Press, 1987.

Fussell, Paul. *The Great War and Modern Memory.* New York: Oxford University Press, 1975.

———. *Wartime: Understanding and Behavior in the Second World War.* New York: Oxford University Press, 1989.

Gallagher, Catherine, and Thomas Laqueur, eds. *The Making of the Modern Body.* Berkeley and Los Angeles: University of California Press, 1987.

Geertz, Clifford. *The Interpretation of Culture.* New York: Basic Books, 1973.

Gibson, James William. *The Perfect War: The War We Couldn't Lose and How We Did.* New York: Vintage Books, 1988.

Gilman, Sander L. *Difference and Pathology: Steretypes of Sexuality, Race, and Madness.* Ithaca, N.Y.: Cornell University Press, 1985.

Gitlin, Tod. *Inside Primetime.* New York: Pantheon Books, 1985.

———. *The Whole World Is Watching: Mass Media and the Unmaking of the New Left.* Berkeley and Los Angeles: University of California Press, 1980.

Gledhill, Christine. *Home Is Where the Heart Is: Studies in Melodrama and the Women's Film.* London: British Film Institute, 1987.

Goldman, Eric F. *The Tragedy of Lyndon Johnson.* New York: Dell, 1969.

Goodwin, Richard N. *Remembering America: A Voice from the Sixties.* Boston: Little, Brown, 1988.

———. *Triumph or Tragedy: Reflections on Vietnam.* New York: Random House, 1966.

Gouldner, Alvin W. *The Future of Intellectuals and the Rise of the New Class.* New York: Seabury Press, 1979.

Gramsci, Antonio. *Selections from Political Writing, 1921–26.* Edited and translated by Quintin Hoare. London: Lawrence & Wishart, 1978.

———. *Selections from the Prison Notebooks.* Edited and translated by Quintin Hoare and Geoffrey Nowell Smith. London: Lawrence & Wishart, 1971.

Grant, Zalin. "Vietnam as Fable." *New Republic,* 25 March 1978, 21–24.

Greene, Graham. *The Quiet American.* Harmondsworth, England: Penguin Books, 1986.

Gunn, Giles. *The Culture of Criticism and the Criticism of Culture.* New York: Oxford University Press, 1987.

Gurevitch, Michael, et al. *Culture, Society, and the Media.* London: Methuen, 1982.

Halberstam, David. *The Best and the Brightest.* Greenwich, Conn.: Faucett, 1972.

——. *The Making of a Quagmire.* New York: Random House, 1964.

——. *One Very Hot Day.* Boston: Houghton Mifflin, 1969. Reprint. New York: Warner Books, 1984.

Hall, Stuart. "Cultural Studies: Two Paradigms." In *Culture, Ideology, and Social Process: A Reader,* edited by Tony Bennett et al., 19–37. London: Billings, Open University Press, 1981.

——. "Notes on Deconstructing the Popular." In *People's History and Socialist Theory,* edited by Raphael Samuel, 227–40. London: Routledge, 1981.

——. "On Postmodernism and Articulation: An Interview with Stuart Hall." *Journal of Communication Inquiry* 10, no. 2 (Summer 1986): 45–60.

Hall, Stuart, et al. *Culture, Media, Language: Working Papers in Cultural Studies, 1972–1979.* London: Hutchinson, 1980.

——. *Policing the Crisis: Mugging, the State, and Law and Order.* London: Macmillan, 1978.

Hammond, Charles Montgomery, Jr. *The Image Decade: Television Documentary, 1965–1975.* New York: Hastings House, 1981.

Harris, Marvin. *Cultural Materialism: The Struggle for a Science of Culture.* New York: Vintage Books, 1980.

Hasford, Gustav. *The Short Timers.* New York: Bantam Books, 1985.

Hayden, Tom. *Reunion: A Memoir.* New York: Random House, 1988.

Heilbronn, Lisa M. "Coming Home a Hero: The Changing Image of the Vietnam Vet on Prime Time Television." *Journal of Popular Film and Television* 13, no. 1 (Spring 1985): 25–30.

Hellmann, John. *American Myth and the Legacy of Vietnam.* New York: Columbia University Press, 1986.

Herr, Michael. *Dispatches.* New York: Knopf, 1977. Reprint. New York: Avon Books, 1980.

Herring, George. *America's Longest War: The United States and Vietnam, 1950–1975.* New York: Wiley, 1979.

Hoberman, J. "The Fascist Guns in the West." *American Film* 11 (March 1986): 42–48.

Hoopes, Townsend. *The Limits of Intervention.* New York: McKay, 1969.

Huber, Richard M. "A Theory of American Studies." *Social Education* 13 (October 1954): 267–71.

Huggett, William Turner. *Body Count.* New York: Putnam, 1973.

Jameson, Fredric. "Postmodernism; or, The Cultural Logic of Late Capitalism." *New Left Review* no. 146 (July-August, 1984): 53–92.

———. "Reification and Utopia in Mass Culture." *Social Text* 1 (1979): 130–48.

Jason, Philip K. *Fourteen Landing Zones: Approaches to Vietnam War Literature.* Iowa City: University of Iowa Press, 1991.

Jeffords, Susan. "Friendly Civilians: Images of Woman and the Feminization of the Audience in Vietnam Films." *Wide Angle* 7, no. 4 (1985): 13–22.

———. *The Remasculinization of America: Gender and the Vietnam War.* Bloomington: Indiana University Press, 1989.

Kadushin, Charles. *The American Intellectual Elite.* Boston: Little, Brown, 1974.

Kagan, Norman. *The War Film: A Pyramid Illustrated History of the Movies.* New York: Pyramid, 1974.

Kagan, Robert W. "Realities and Myths of the Vietnam War." *Wall Street Journal,* 1 April 1982, 1.

Kaplan, Peter W. "The End of the Soft Line: A Guide to the New Hard-Line Culture." *Esquire,* April 1980, 41–44.

Karnow, Stanley. *Vietnam: A History.* New York: Viking Press, 1983.

Kattenberg, Paul M. *Vietnam: Trauma in American Foreign Policy.* New Brunswick, N.J.: Transaction Books, 1980.

Katz, Seymour. "Culture and Literature in American Studies." *American Quarterly* 20, no. 3 (Summer 1968): 318–29.

Kauffman, Stanley. "The Hunting of the Hunters: Vietnam." *New Republic,* 26 May 1979, 22–23.

———. "Tell the Real Lies: Films about Vietnam." *New Republic,* 2 March 1968, 26.

Kazin, Alfred. "Vietnam: It Was US against Us." *Esquire,* March 1978, 120–23.

Kellner, Douglas. "T.V., Ideology, and Emancipatory Popular Culture." *Socialist Review* 45 (1979): 13–53.

Kelly, R. Gordon. "Literature and the Historian." *American Quarterly* 26 (May 1974): 141–59.

Kendrick, Alexander. *The Wound Within: America in the Vietnam Years, 1954–1974.* Boston: Little, Brown, 1974.

Kerber, Linda K. "Diversity and the Transformation of American Studies." *American Quarterly* 41, no. 3 (September 1989): 415–31.

Kerr, Paul. "The Vietnam Subtext." *Screen* 21, no. 2 (1980): 67–72.

Kinder, Marsha. "The Power of Adaptation in *Apocalypse Now.*" *Film Quarterly* 33, no. 2 (Winter 1979–80): 12–20.

————. "Political Game." *Film Quarterly* 32, no. 4 (Summer 1979): 13–17.

Kinney, Judy Lee. "The Mythical Method: Fictionalizing the Vietnam War." *Wide Angle* 7, no. 4 (1985): 35–40.

Klare, Michael T. *Beyond the Vietnam Syndrome: U.S. Interventionism in the 1980s.* Washington, D.C.: Washington Institute for Policy Studies, 1981.

————. "Curing the Vietnam Syndrome." *The Nation*, 13 October 1979, 337–40.

Kolodny, Annette. *The Lay of the Land: Metaphor as Experience and History in American Life and Letters.* Chapel Hill: University of North Carolina Press, 1975.

Kolko, Gabriel. *Roots of American Foreign Policy.* Boston: Beacon Press, 1969.

Kovic, Ron. *Born on the Fourth of July.* New York: McGraw-Hill, 1976. Reprint, New York: Pocket Books, 1977.

Kroeber, A. L., and Clyde Kluckhohn. *Culture: A Critical Review of Concepts and Methods.* Cambridge: Harvard University Press, 1952.

Krupnick, Mark. *Lionel Trilling and the Fate of Cultural Criticism.* Evanston, Ill.: Northwestern University Press, 1986.

Kuberski, Philip Francis. "Genres of Vietnam." *Cultural Critique* 3 (Spring 1986): 168–88.

Kuklick, Bruce. "Myth and Symbol in American Studies." *American Quarterly* 24, no. 4 (October 1972): 435–50.

Kwiat, Joseph J., and Mary C. Turpie. *Studies in American Culture: Dominant Ideas and Images.* Minneapolis: University of Minnesota Press, 1960.

Ladd, Everett Carll, Jr., and Seymour Lipsett. *Academics, Politics, and the 1972 Election.* Washington, D.C.: American Enterprise Institute for Policy Research, 1973.

LaFaber, Walter. "The Last War, the Next War, and the New Revisionists." *Democracy* 1, no. 1 (January 1981): 93–103.

Lasch, Christopher. *The Culture of Narcissism: American Life in an Age of Diminishing Expectations.* New York: Norton, 1978.

————. "Mass Culture Reconsidered." *Democracy* 1, no. 4 (October 1981): 7–22.

————. *The New Radicalism in America, 1889–1963.* New York: Norton, 1965.

Lazere, Donald. *American Media and Mass Culture: Left Perspectives.* Berkeley and Los Angeles: University of California Press, 1987.

————. "Mass Culture, Political Consciousness, and English Studies." *College English* 38, no. 8 (April 1977): 751–67.

Leitch, Vincent B. *American Literary Criticism: From the Thirties to the Eighties.* New York: Columbia University Press, 1988.

Lewy, Guenter. *America in Vietnam.* New York: Oxford University Press, 1978.

Lomperis, Timothy J. *Reading the Wind: The Literature of the Vietnam War.* Durham, N.C.: Duke University Press, 1987.

Lovell, Terry. *Pictures of Reality: Aesthetics, Politics, and Pleasure.* London: British Film Institute, 1980.

Luedtke, Luther S., ed. *The Study of American Culture: The Contemporary Conflicts.* Deland, Fla.: Evertt, Edwards, 1977.

MacCabe, Colin. "Realism and the Cinema: Notes on Some Brechtian Theses." *Screen* 15, no. 2 (Summer 1974): 9–15.

McCarthy, Todd, and Todd Flynn, eds. *King of the B's: Working within the Hollywood System.* New York: Dutton, 1975.

MacDonald, J. Fred. "The Cold War as Entertainment in Fifties Television." *Journal of Popular Film and Television* 7, no. 1 (1978): 3–31.

———. *Television and the Red Menace: The Video Road to Vietnam.* New York: Praeger, 1985.

McDowell, Tremaine. *American Studies.* Minneapolis: University of Minnesota Press, 1948.

Macherey, Pierre. *A Theory of Literary Production.* Translated by Geoffrey Wall. London: Routledge and Kegan Paul, 1978.

McInerey, Peter. "Apocalypse Then: Hollywood Looks Back at Vietnam." *Film Quarterly* 33, no. 2 (Winter 1979–80): 21–32.

McMahany, Jeff. *Reagan and the World: Imperial Policy in the New Cold War.* London: Pluto, 1984.

MacPherson, Myra. *Long Time Passing: Vietnam and the Haunted Generation.* Garden City, N.Y.: Doubleday, 1984.

Mailer, Norman. *Why Are We in Vietnam: A Novel.* New York: Putnam, 1967.

Marcus, Griel. *Mystery Train: Images of America in Rock 'n' Roll Music.* New York: Dutton, 1976.

Marin, Peter. "Coming to Terms with Vietnam." *Harpers,* December 1980, 41–56.

———. "Rerunning the War." *Mother Jones,* November 1983, 11–16.

Martin, Andrew, and Patrice Petro. "An Interview with Terry Eagleton." *Social Text* 11–12 (Winter-Spring, 1986–87): 83–99.

Marx, Leo. "American Studies: A Defense of an Unscientific Method." *New Literary History* 1 (Fall 1969): 75–90.

———. "Thoughts on the Origin and Character of the American Studies Movement." *American Quarterly* 31, no. 3 (Fall 1979): 398–401.

Mason, Bobbie Ann. *In Country.* New York: Harper & Row, 1985.

Mechling, Jay, et al. "American Cultural Studies: The Discipline and the Curriculum." *American Quarterly* 25, no. 4 (October 1973): 363–89.

Merideth, Robert, ed. *American Studies: Essays on Theory and Method.* Columbus, Ohio: Merrill, 1968.

Mertz, Robert J., and Michael T. Marsden. "American Culture Studies: A Discipline in Search of Itself." *Journal of Popular Culture* 9 (Fall 1975): 461–70.

Michaels, Walter Benn, and Donald Pease. *The American Renaissance Reconsidered.* Baltimore: John Hopkins University Press, 1985.

Mills, Nicolaus. "Memories of the Vietnam War." *Dissent* (Summer 1979): 334–37.

Mithers, Carol Lynn. "Missing in Action: Women Warriors in Vietnam." *Cultural Critique* 3 (Spring 1986): 79–90.

Moore, Roger. *The Green Berets.* New York: Avon Books, 1965.

Morris, Meaghan, "Banality in Cultural Studies." *Discourse* 10, no. 2 (Spring-Summer 1988): 3–29.

Murray, Lawrence L. "Hollywood, Nihilism, and the Youth Culture of the Sixties: *Bonnie and Clyde.*" In *American History/American Film,* edited by John E. O'Connor and Martin A. Jackson, 237–56. New York: Ungar, 1980.

Myers, Thomas. *Walking Point: American Narratives of the Vietnam War.* New York: Oxford University Press, 1988.

Newman, John. *Vietnam War Literature.* Metuchen, N.J.: Scarecrow Press, 1982.

Norden, Martin F. "The Disabled Vietnam Veteran in Hollywood Films." *Journal of Popular Film and Television* 11, no. 4 (Winter 1984): 145–51.

O'Brien, Tim. *Going after Cacciato.* New York: Delacorte Press, 1978. Reprint. New York: Dell, 1980.

———. *The Things They Carried.* New York: Penguin Books, 1990.

———. "The Violent Vets." *Esquire,* December 1979, 96–104.

O'Connor, John, ed. *American History/American Television: Interpreting the Video Past.* New York: Ungar, 1983.

O'Hallaren, Bill. "It's Back to the Beach for Dana Delany." *TV Guide,* 16–22 June 1990, 10–13.

O'Neil, William L. *Coming Apart: An Informal History of American in the Sixties.* Chicago: Quadrangle, 1971.

Ortner, Sherry B. "Theory in Anthropology since the Sixties." *Comparative Studies in Society and History* 26 (January 1984): 126–66.

Parker, Maynard. "Vietnam: The War That Won't End." *Foreign Affairs* 53, no. 2 (January 1975): 352–74.

Pearce, Roy Harvey. "American Studies as a Discipline." *College English* 18, no. 4 (January 1957): 179–86.

Pecheux, Michel. *Language, Semantics and Ideology: Stating the Obvious.* Translated by Harbans Nagpal. London: Macmillan, 1982.

Pelfrey, William. *The Big V.* New York: Liveright, 1972.

———. "Face Down: Climax to the Hardship Tour." *New Republic,* 18 July 1970, 13–14.

Perret, Geoffrey. *A Country Made by War: From the Revolution to Vietnam: The Story of America's Rise to Power.* New York: Random House, 1989.

Podhoretz, Norman. *Breaking Ranks: A Political Memoir.* New York: Harper & Row, 1979.

———. *Why We Were in Vietnam.* New York: Simon & Schuster, 1982.

Puhr, Kathleen M. "Four Faces of the Vietnam War." *Modern Fiction Studies* 30, no. 1 (Spring 1984): 99–117.

Quart, Leonard, and Albert Auster. *American Film and Society since 1945.* New York: Praeger, 1984.

———. *How the War Was Remembered.* New York: Praeger, 1988.

———. "The Wounded Vet in Post-War Film." *Social Policy* 13, no. 2 (Fall 1982): 24–31.

Real, Michael R. *Mass-Mediated Culture.* Englewood Cliffs, N.J.: Prentice-Hall, 1977.

Reich, Charles A. *The Greening of America.* New York: Random House, 1970.

Roddick, Nick. *A New Deal in Entertainment: Warner Brothers in the 1930s.* London: British Film Institute, 1983

Ross, Andrew, *No Respect: Intellectuals and Popular Culture.* New York: Routledge, 1989.

Roszac, Theodore. *The Dissenting Academy.* New York: Pantheon Books, 1968.

———. *The Making of a Counter Culture: Reflections on the Technocratic Society and Its Youthful Opposition.* New York: Anchor Books, 1969.

Roth, Mark. "Some Warners Musicals and the Spirit of the New Deal." In *Genre: The Musical,* edited by Rick Altman, 41–56. London: British Film Institute, 1982.

Rowe, John Carlos. "Bringing It All Back Home: American Recycling of the Vietnam War," Working Paper no. 3, Center for Twentieth-Century Studies, University of Wisconsin at Milwaukee, Fall 1988. Reprinted in Nancy *The Violence of Representation: Literature and the History of Violence,* edited by Nancy Armstrong and Leonard Tennenhouse, 197–218. New York: Routledge, 1989.

182   WORKS CITED

—. "Eye-Witness: Documentary Styles in the American Representations of Vietnam." *Cultural Critique* 3 (Spring 1986): 126–50.

Ryan, Michael, and Douglas Kellner. *Camera Politica: The Politics and Ideology of Contemporary Hollywood.* Bloomington: Indiana University Press, 1990.

Said, Edward. *The World, The Text, and The Critic.* Cambridge: Harvard University Press, 1983.

Santoli, Al. *Everything We Had.* New York: Random House, 1981.

Sarris, Andrew. "The Screen at the End of the Tunnel." *Village Voice,* 8 September 1987, 19, 26, 28–29, 54.

Sassoon, Anne Showstack. *Gramsci's Politics.* Minneapolis: University of Minnesota Press, 1987.

Sayre, Nora. *Running Time: Films of the Cold War.* New York: Dial Press, 1982.

Sayres, Sohnya, et al., eds. *The 60s without Apologies.* Minneapolis: University of Minnesota Press, 1984.

Schlesinger, Arthur M., Jr. *The Bitter Heritage: Vietnam and American Democracy.* Boston: Houghton Mifflin, 1966.

Schlissel, Lillian, ed. *The World of Randolph Bourne.* Boston: Houghton Mifflin, 1967.

Scruggs, Jan C., and Joel L. Swerdlow. *To Heal a Nation: The Vietnam Veterans Memorial.* New York: Harper & Row, 1985.

Shawcross, William. *Sideshow: Kissinger, Nixon, and the Destruction of Cambodia.* New York: Simon & Schuster, 1979.

Sheehan, Neil. *A Bright Shining Lie: John Paul Vann and America in Vietnam.* New York: Random House, 1988.

Sklar, Robert. "American Studies and the Realities of American Culture." *American Quarterly* 22, no. 2 (Summer 1970): 597–605.

—. "The Problems of an American Studies Philosophy: A Bibliography of New Directions." *American Quarterly* 27, no. 2 (Summer 1975): 245–62.

Sloan, James Park. *War Games.* Boston: Houghton Mifflin, 1971.

Sloterdijk, Peter. *Critique of Cynical Reasoning.* Translated by Michael Eldred. Minneapolis: University of Minnesota Press, 1987.

Slotkin, Richard. *The Fatal Environment: The Myth of the Frontier in the Age of Industrialization, 1800–1890.* Middletown, Conn.: Wesleyan University Press, 1986.

—. "Gunfighters and Green Berets: The Magnificent Seven and the Myth of Counter-Insurgency." *Radical History* 44 (Spring 1989): 64–90.

—. *Regeneration through Violence: The Mythology of the American Frontier, 1600–1860.* Middletown, Conn.: Wesleyan University Press, 1973.

Smith, Claude J., Jr. "The Rehabilitation of the U.S. Military in Films since 1978." *Journal of Popular Films and Television* 11, no. 4 (Winter 1984): 145–51.

Smith, Henry Nash. "Can American Studies Develop a Method?" *American Quarterly* 9 (Summer 1957). Reprinted in *Studies in American Culture: Dominant Ideas and Images*, edited by Joseph J. Kwiat and Mary C. Turpie, 12–20. Minneapolis: University of Minnesota Press, 1960.

———. *Virgin Land: The American West as Symbol and Myth.* Cambridge: Harvard University Press, 1970.

Smith, Julian. *Looking Away: Hollywood and Vietnam.* New York: Scribner, 1975.

Sontag, Susan. "Fascinating Fascism." *New York Review of Books*, 6 February 1975. Reprint in *Movies and Methods*, edited by Bill Nichols, 31–43. Berkeley and Los Angeles: University of California Press, 1976.

Sontag, Susan. "The Imagination of Disaster," *Commentary* 40 (October 1965): 42–48.

Spark, Alasdair. "The Soldier at the Heart of the War: The Myth of the Green Beret in the Popular Culture of the Vietnam Era." *Journal of American Studies* 18, no. 1 (April 1984): 29–48.

Springer, Claudia. "Military Propaganda: Defense Department Films from World War II and Vietnam." *Cultural Critique* 3 (Spring 1986): 151–67.

Stanton, M. Duncan, and Charles R. Figley. *Stress Disorders among Vietnam Veterans.* New York: Brunner, Mazel, 1978.

Starr, Paul. *The Discarded Army: Veterans after Vietnam.* New York: Charterhouse, 1973.

Steel, Ronald. *Walter Lippmann and the American Century.* New York: Vintage Books, 1981.

Stephanson, Anders. "Interview with Cornel West." In *Universal Abandon: The Politics of Postmodernism*, edited by Andrew Ross, 269–86. Minneapolis: University of Minnesota Press, 1988.

Stolz, Matthew, ed. *The Politics of the New Left.* Beverly Hills, Cal.: Glencoe Press, 1971.

Suid, Lawrence H. *Guts and Glory: Great American War Movies.* Reading, Mass.: Addison-Wesley, 1978.

Susman, Warren I. *Culture as History: The Transformation of American Society in the Twentieth Century.* New York: Pantheon Books, 1984.

Sykes, Richard E. "American Studies and the Concept of Culture: A Theory and Method." *American Quarterly* 15, no. 2 (Summer 1963): 253–70.

Tate, Cecil F. *The Search for a Method in American Studies.* Minneapolis: University of Minnesota Press, 1973.

Taylor, Clyde, ed. *Vietnam and Black America: An Anthology of Protest and Resistance.* New York: Anchor Books, 1973.

Taylor, Gordon O. "American Personal Narrative of the War in Vietnam." *American Literature* 52 (1980): 294–308.

Terry, Wallace. *Bloods: An Oral History of the Vietnam War by Black Veterans.* New York: Random House, 1984.

Theweleit, Klaus. *Male Fantasies.* Volume I, *Women, Floods, Bodies, History.* Minneapolis: University of Minnesota Press, 1987.

Trachtenberg, Alan. *The Incorporation of America: Culture and Society in the Gilded Age.* New York: Hill & Wang, 1982.

Turner, Kathleen J. *Lyndon Johnson's Dual War: Vietnam and the Press.* Chicago: University of Chicago Press, 1985.

Ungar, Irwin. *The Movement: A History of the American New Left, 1959–1972.* New York: Wiley, 1974.

Virilio, Paul. *War and Cinema: The Logistics of Perception.* Translated by Patrick Camiller. London: Verso, 1984.

Vogelgesang, Sandy. *The Long Dark Night of the Soul: The American Intellectual Left and the Vietnam War.* New York: Harper & Row, 1974.

Walker, Robert. *American Studies in the United States: A Survey of Programs.* Baton Rouge: Louisiana State University Press, 1958.

Walzer, Michael. "Were We Wrong about Vietnam?" *New Republic,* 18 August 1979, 15.

Webb, James. *Fields of Fire.* Englewood Cliffs, N.J.: Prentice-Hall, 1978.

Westmoreland, General William A. *A Soldier's Report.* Garden City, N.Y.: Doubleday, 1976.

Wheeler, John. *Touched with Fire: The Future of the Vietnam Generation.* New York: Avon Books, 1984.

Williams, John A. *Captain Blackman.* Garden City, N.Y.: Doubleday, 1972.

Williams, Raymond. *Culture and Society, 1780–1950.* New York: Columbia University Press, 1983.

———. *Marxism and Literature.* London: Oxford University Press, 1977.

———. *Politics and Letters: Interviews With New Left Review.* London: Verso, 1981.

———. *Problems in Materialism and Culture.* London: Verso, 1980.

———. *Television: Technology and Cultural Form.* New York: Schocken Books, 1975.

Wilson, James C. *Vietnam in Prose and Film.* Jefferson, N.C.: MacFarland, 1982.

Wise, Gene. "Paradigm Dramas in American Studies: A Cultural and Institutional History of the Movement." *American Quarterly* 31, no. 3 (Fall 1979): 293–337.

Woffard, Harris. *Of Kennedy and Kings: Making Sense of the Sixties.* New York: Farrar, Straus & Giroux, 1980.

Wood, Robin. *Hollywood from Vietnam to Reagan.* New York: Columbia University Press, 1986.

Wright, Will. *Sixguns and Society: A Structural Study of the Western.* Berkeley and Los Angeles: University of California Press, 1975.

INDEX

Thompson, E. P., 27–28, 44
T. J. Hooker, 148
Thompkins, Jane, 31n.12
Top Gun (1986), 123
Tora, Tora, Tora (1970), 109
Tour of Duty, 3–4, 22, 128, 135, 139, 148, 158
Trachtenberg, Alan, 46n.51, 100
Tracks (1977), 104, 138, 146
Trapper John, M. D., 148
Trilling, Lionel, 62
Turner, Frederick Jackson, 101
Tylor, Edward, 34, 45

Ugly American, The (1958), 14–15; *The Quiet American* and, 17. *See also* Lederer, William, and Eugene Berdick
Ulzana's Raid (1972), 105
Uncommon Valor (1983), 125–26

Valente, Jack, 107
Vann, John Paul, 64–65
Veterans Administration, 79
Viet Cong, 73, 79, 82, 84, 100, 105, 108, 115, 139; Rambo as, 125
Vietnamese, 99–100; civilian deaths calculated, 19
Vietnam syndrome, 53, 91, 123, 155–56; as coded referent, 5–6
Vietnam Veterans, 8–9, 55–56, 72, 103, 122, 126, 133, 141, 148, 157–58; in *Coming Home*, 111–12; in *In Country*, 92–93; and popular culture, 79; Rambo and, 52; television drama and, 90
Vietnam Veterans Against the War, 83
Virilio, Paul, 102, 159
Visiters, The (1972), 104

Wagner, Richard, 117
Walker, Robert, 32–34
Wallace, Anthony F. C., 39–41, 46

Warner Brothers, 98
Warren, Robert Penn, 68
Watergate, 10, 50, 110, 120–21
Wayne, John, 79, 86, 109, 138; *The Green Berets* and, 103
Wayne, Michael, 108
Webb, James, 76, 90. *See also Fields of Fire*
West, Cornel, 7
Westerns, 98, 103–104, 141; and *The Green Berets*, 108
Westmoreland, William C., 8, 65
White, Leslie, 33n.18
White House Festival of the Arts (1965), 68
Whole cultural event, Vietnam War as, 23
Who'll Stop the Rain (1978), 138, 146
Wild Bunch, The (1969), 105
Wild in the Streets (1968), 106
Wild West Shows, 101
Williams, Raymond, 27, 47, 52, 54, 113, 143; on concept of masses, 25; critical knowledge, 65; as cultural outsider, 44; culture as selective process, 49; dominant, residual, and emergent elements, 51; on historical changes in culture concept, 45; ideology as lived, 65; official consciousness, 19; on Tylor's concept of culture, 46
Wilson, Woodrow, 66
Wise, Gene, 36–38
Women's Studies, 38
Wood, Robin, 114n.32, 117, 121
Woodstock (1969), 106
World War I, 58
World War II, 12, 23, 34, 36, 66, 69, 88, 109, 130
Wuthnow, Robert, 42n.44

Youth Movement, 32

Zabriski Point (1969), 106